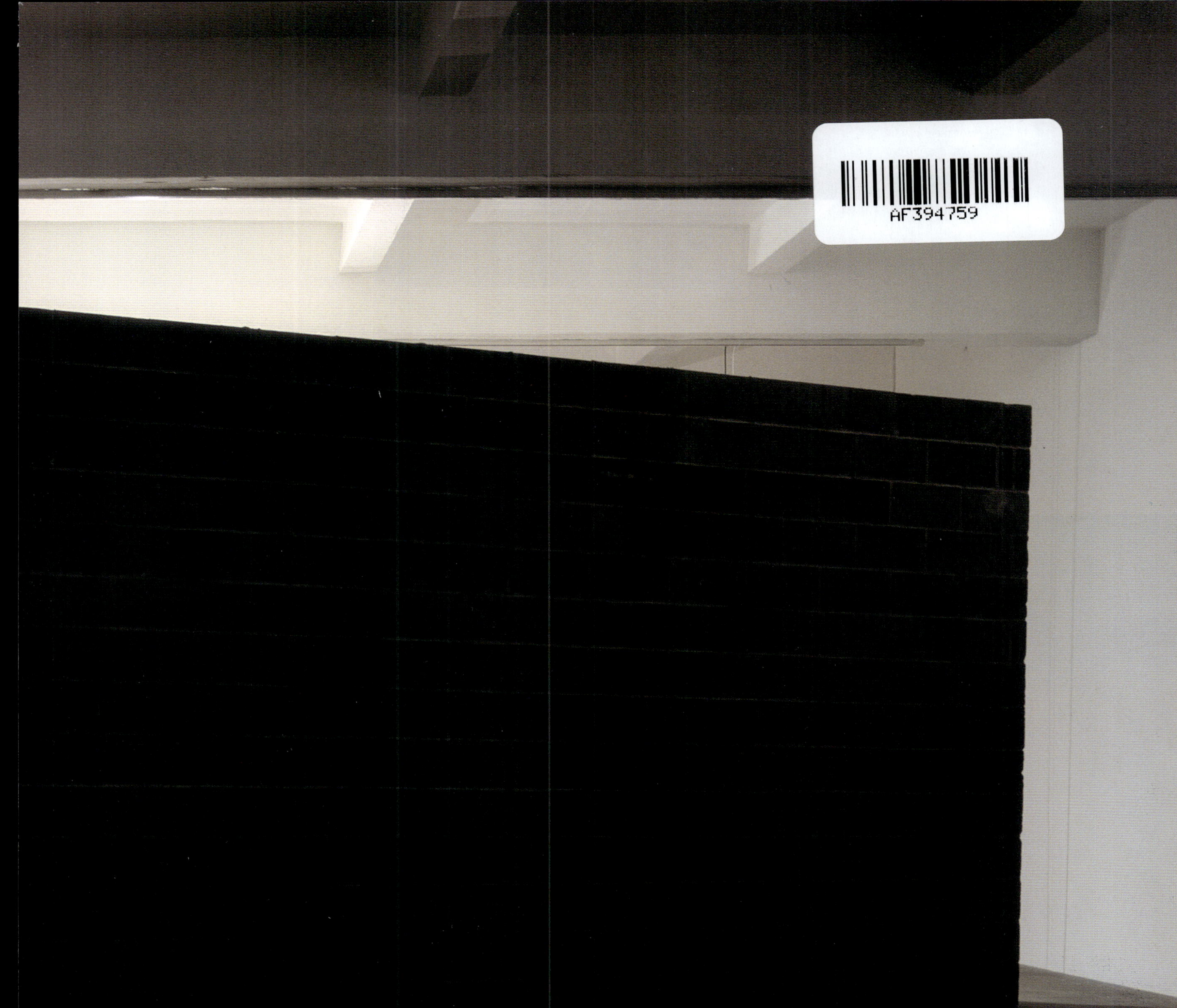
AF394759

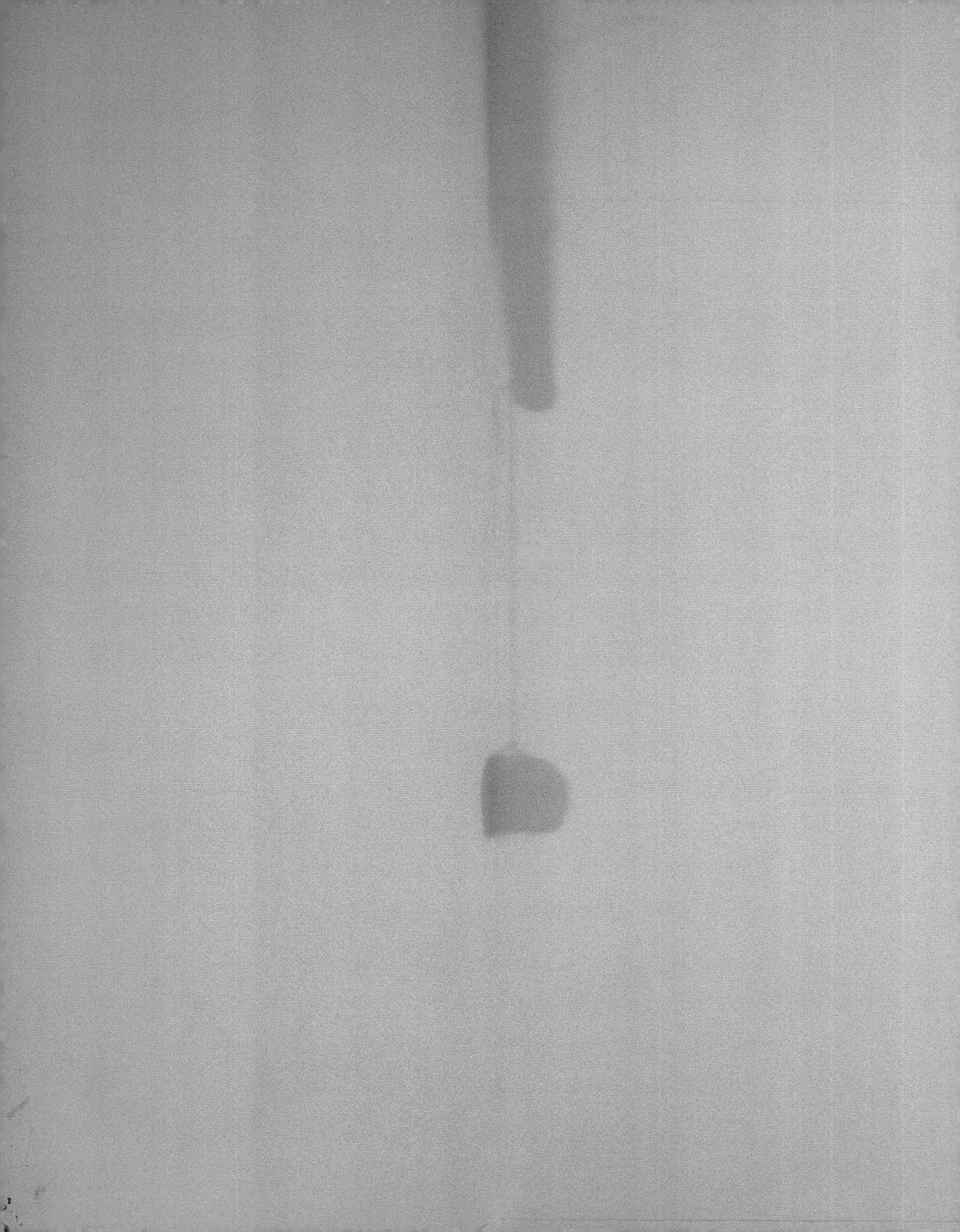

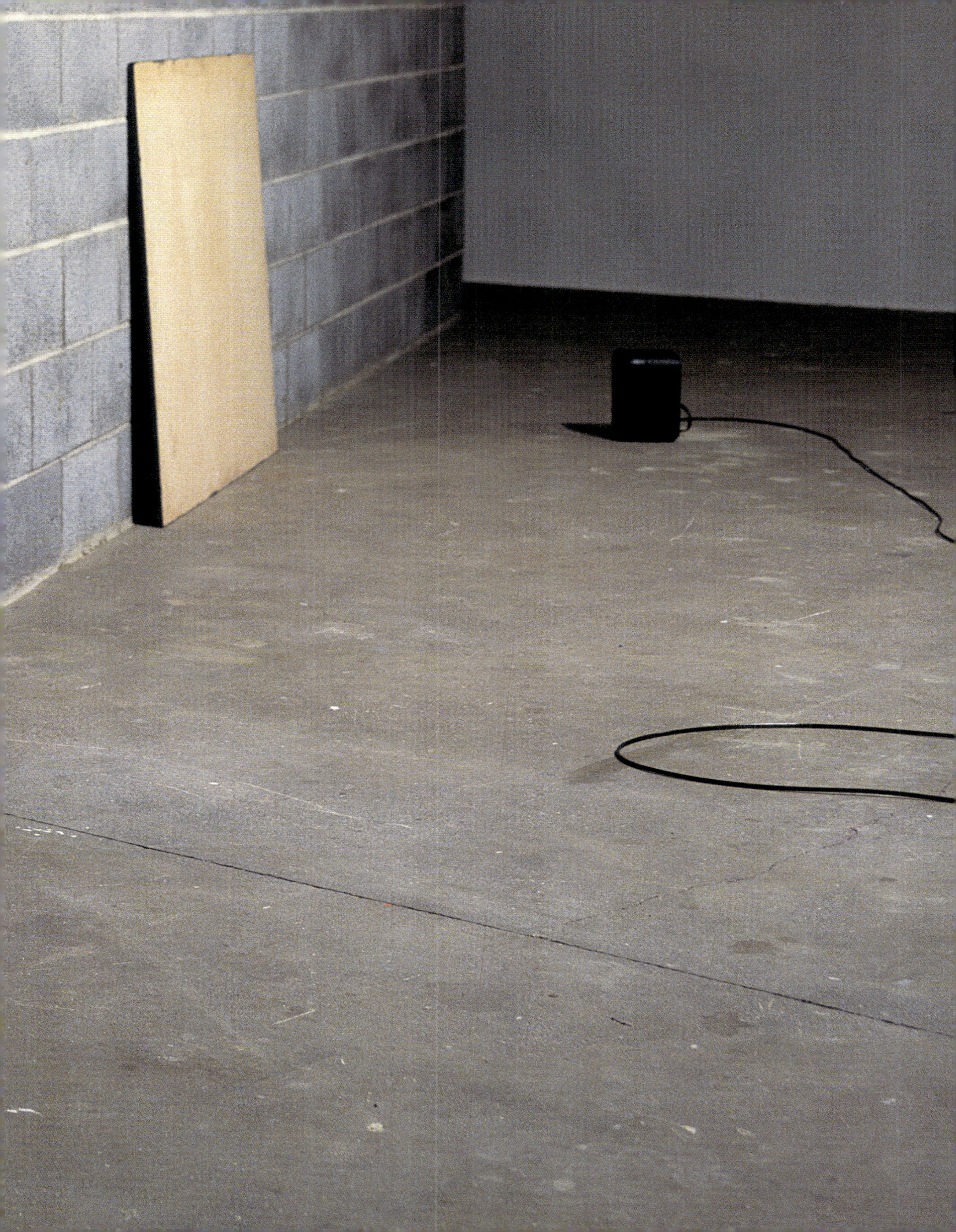

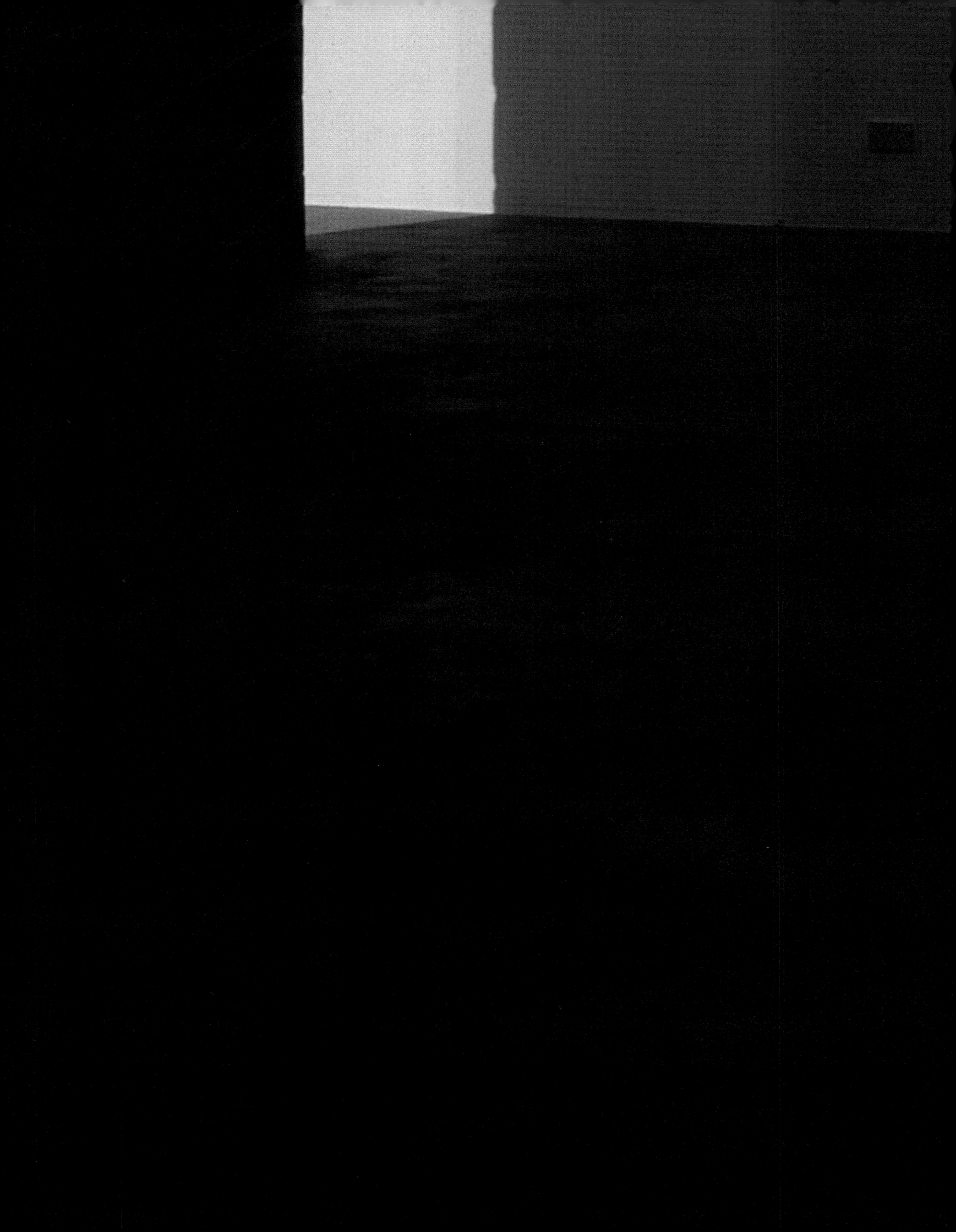

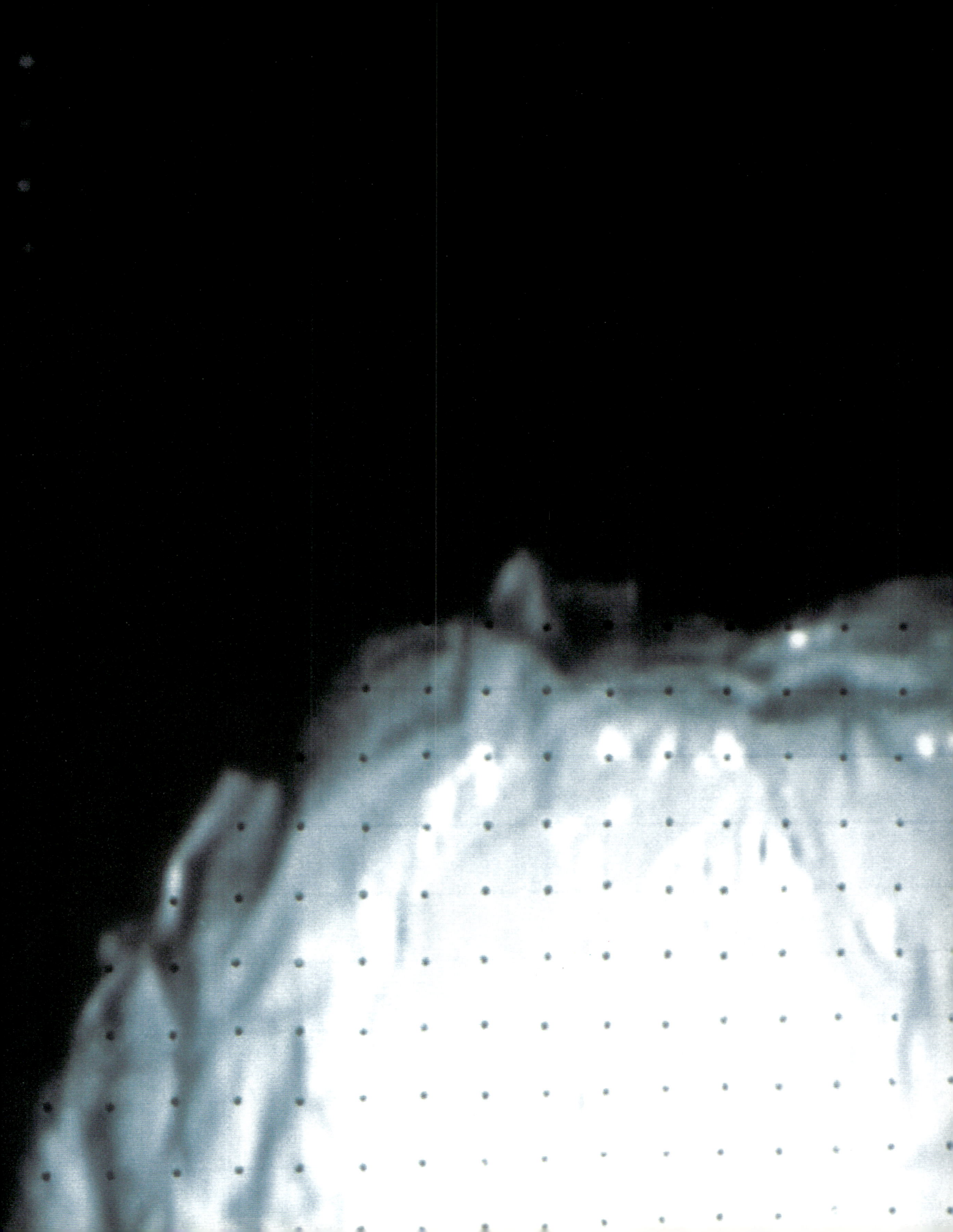

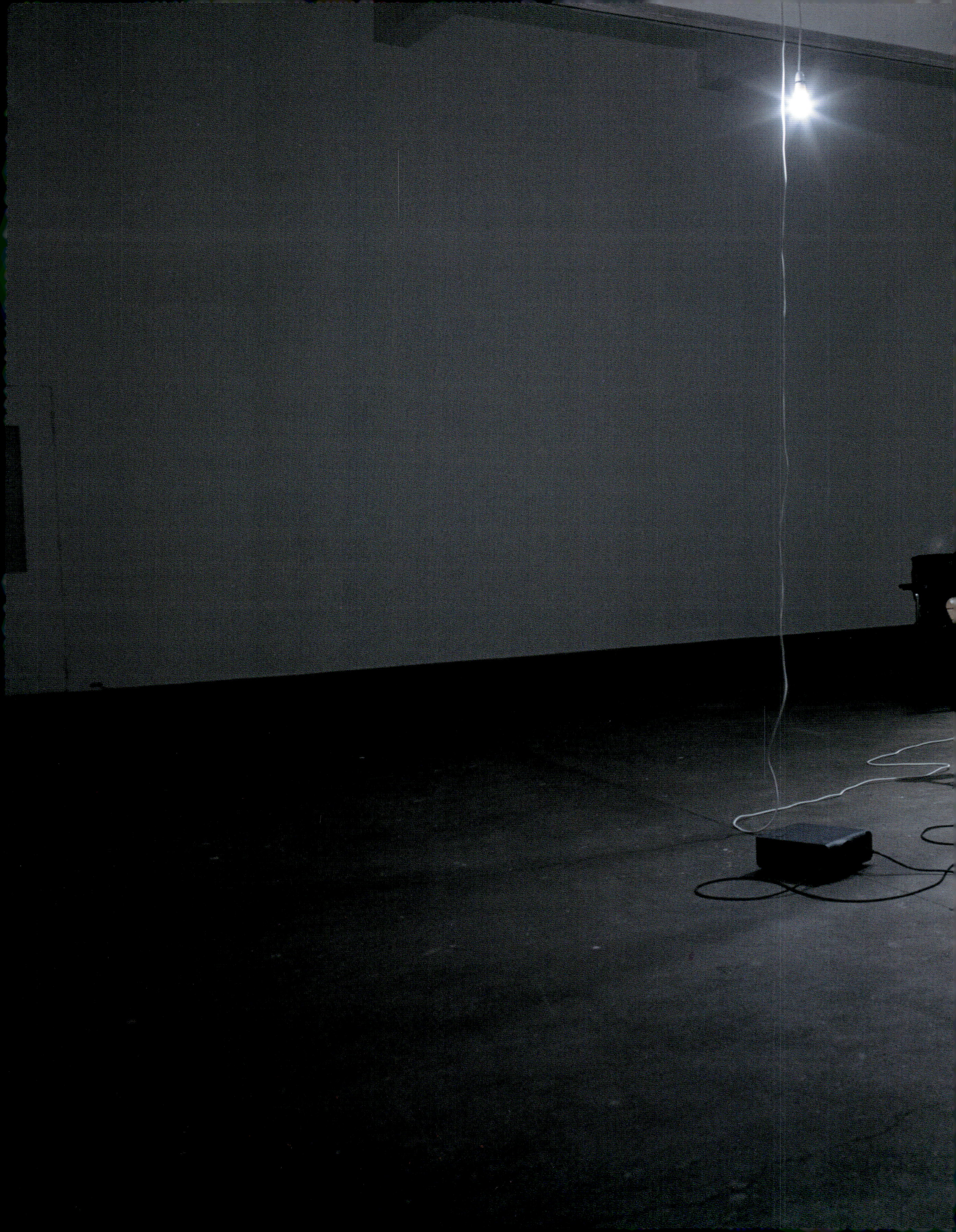

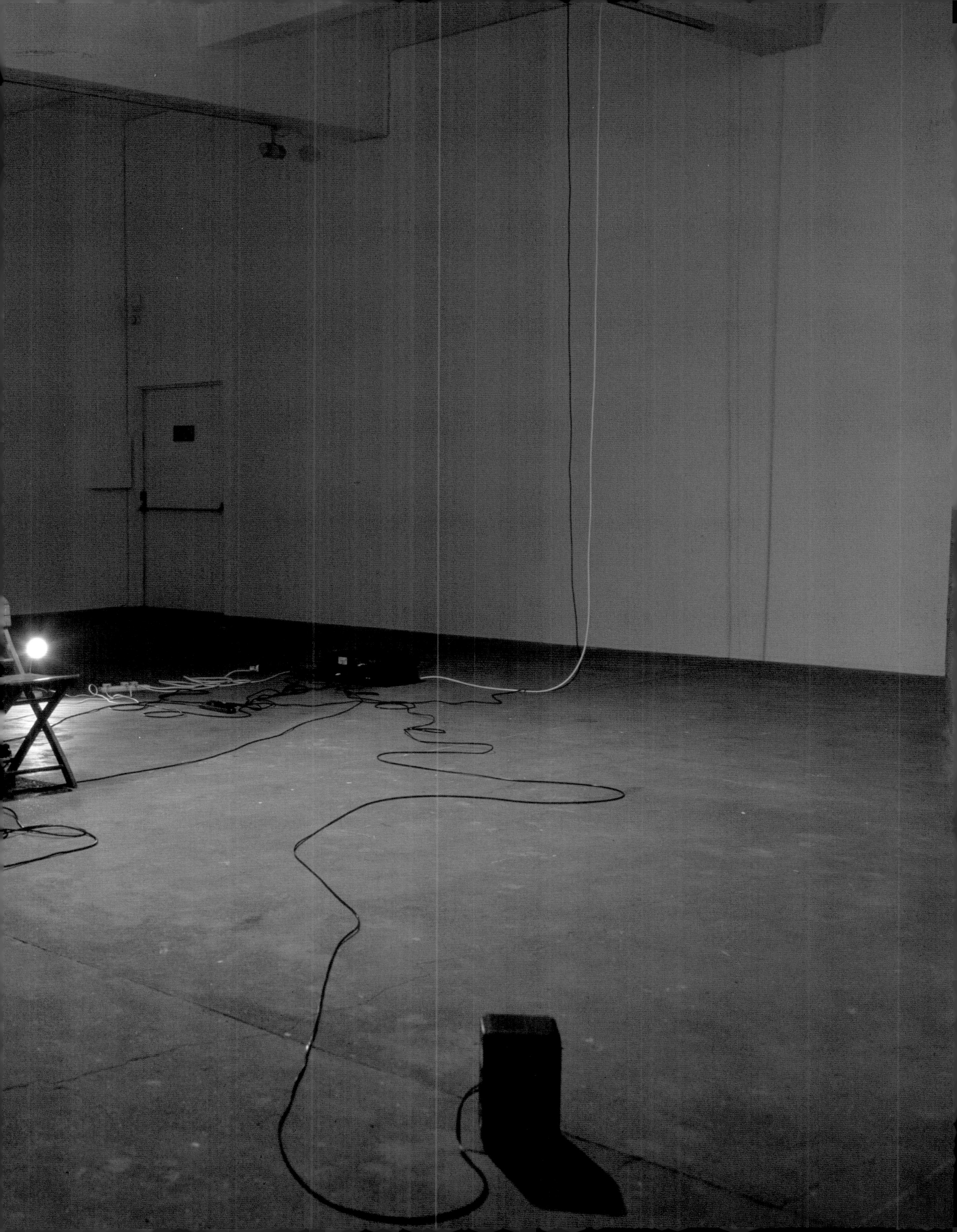

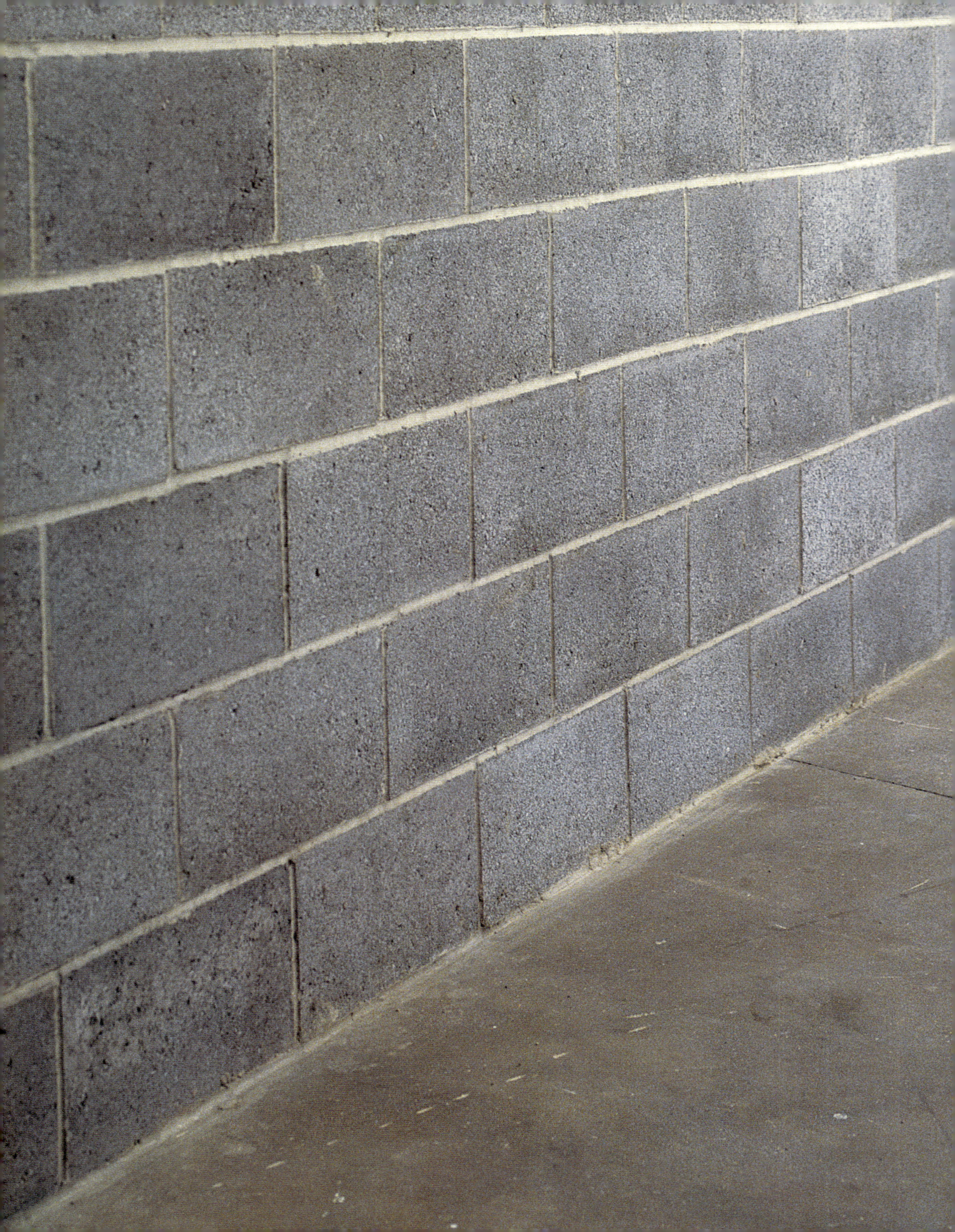

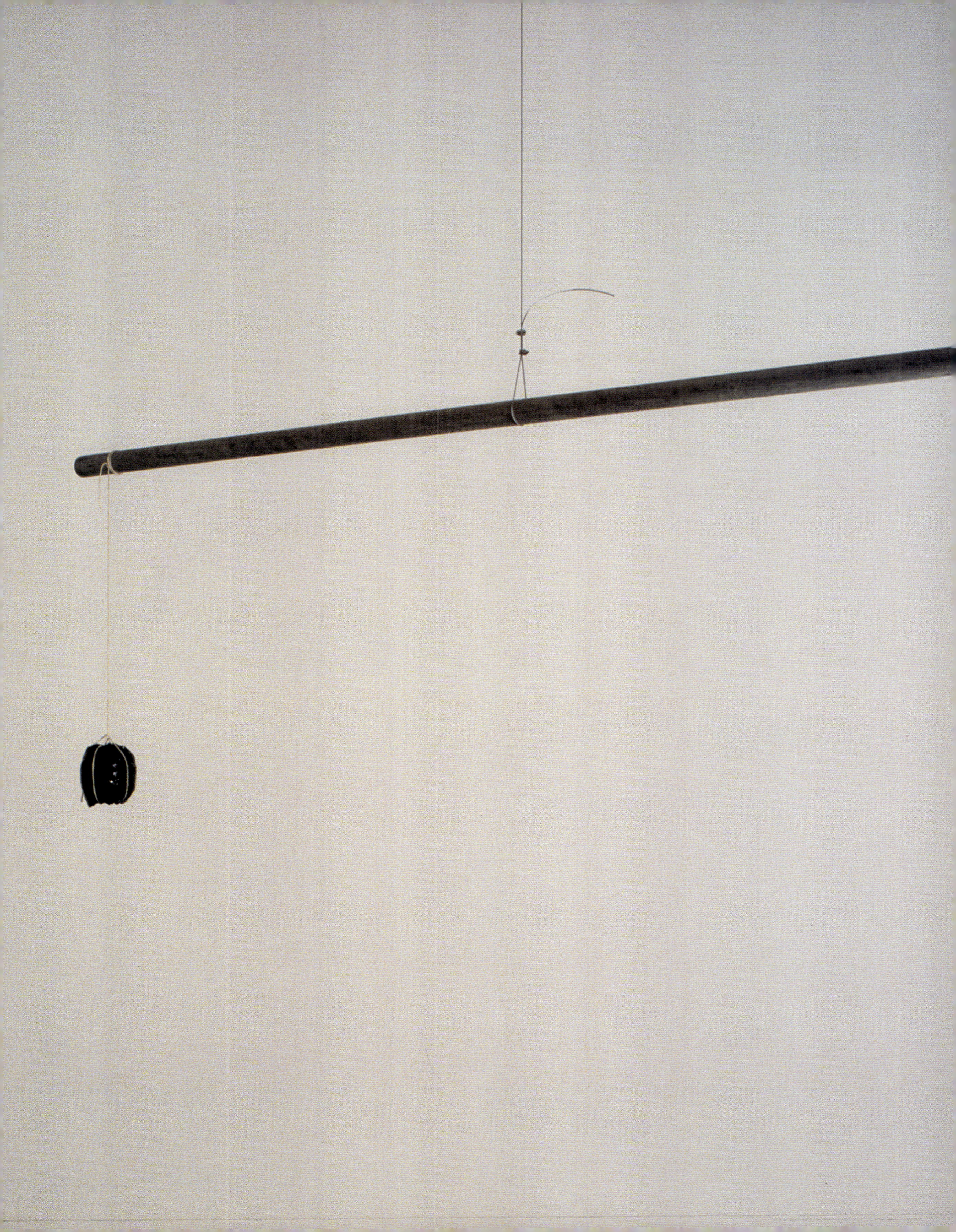

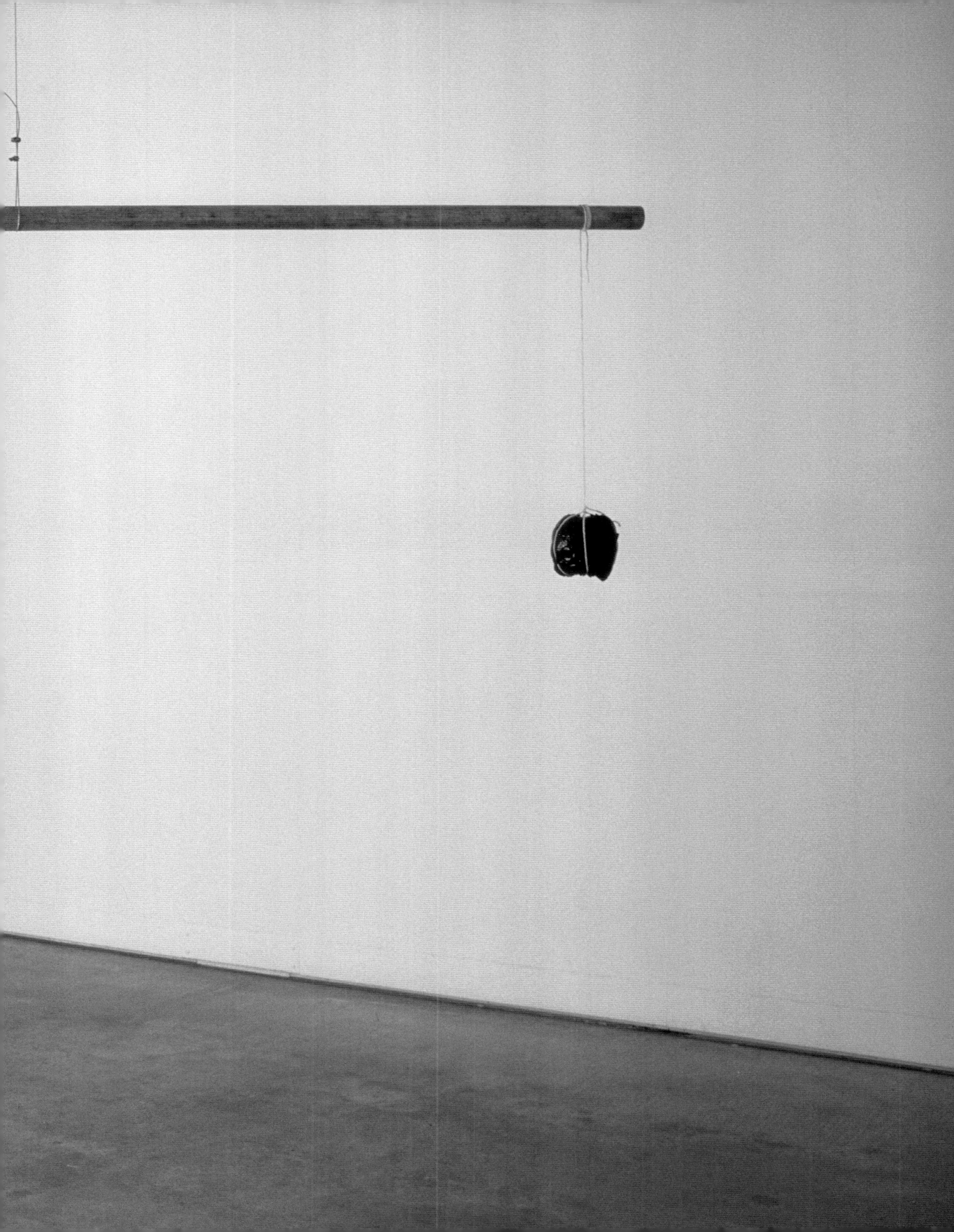

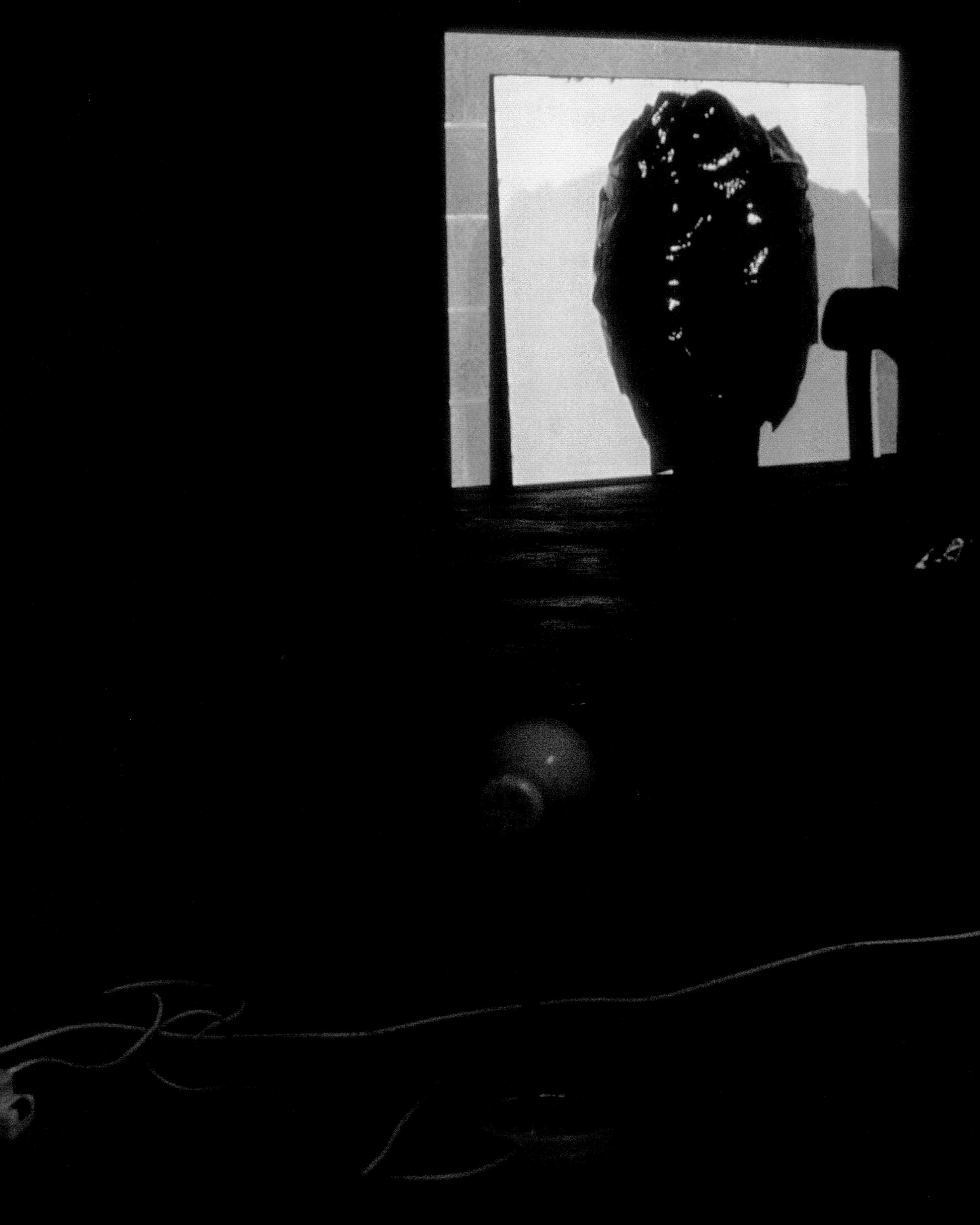

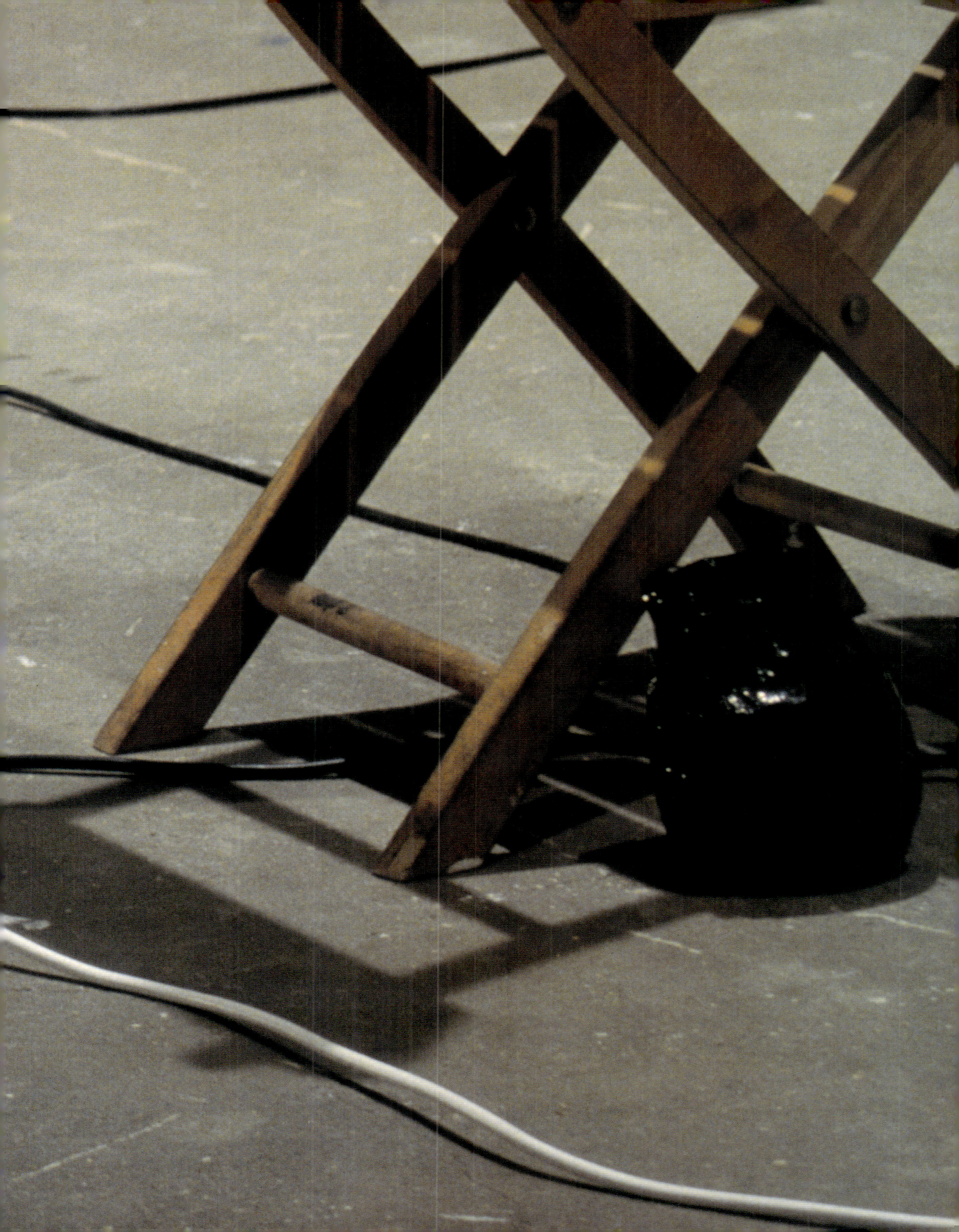

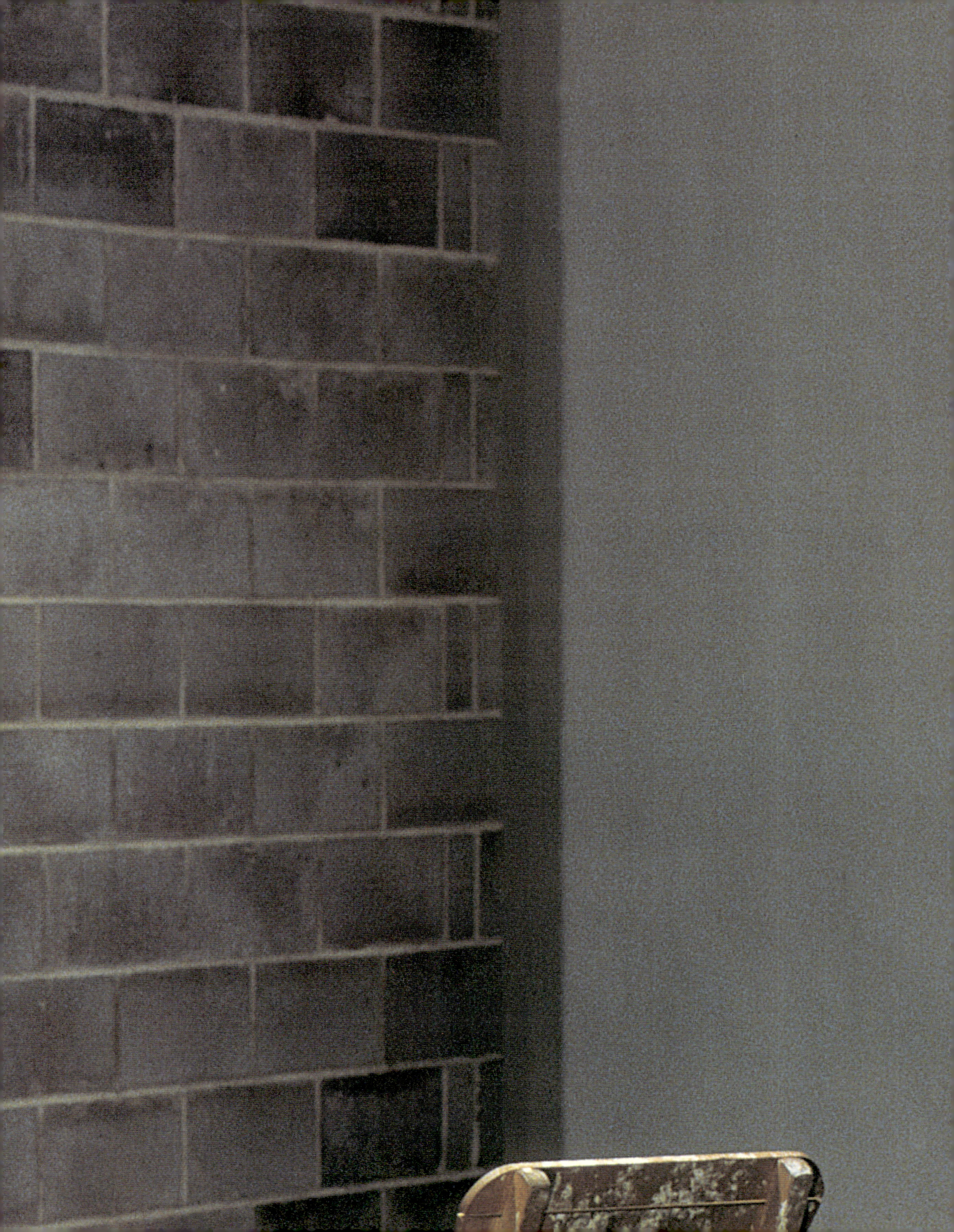

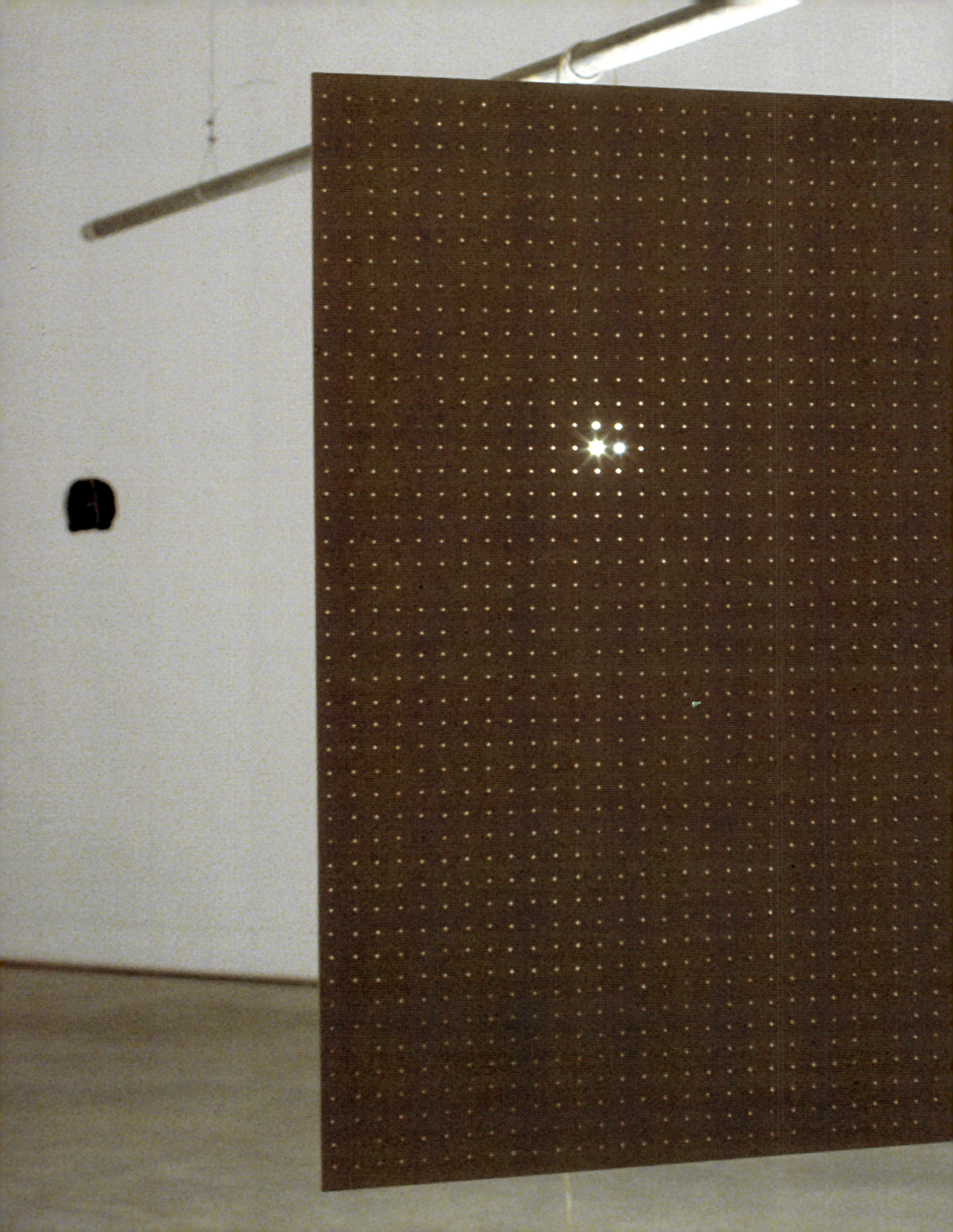

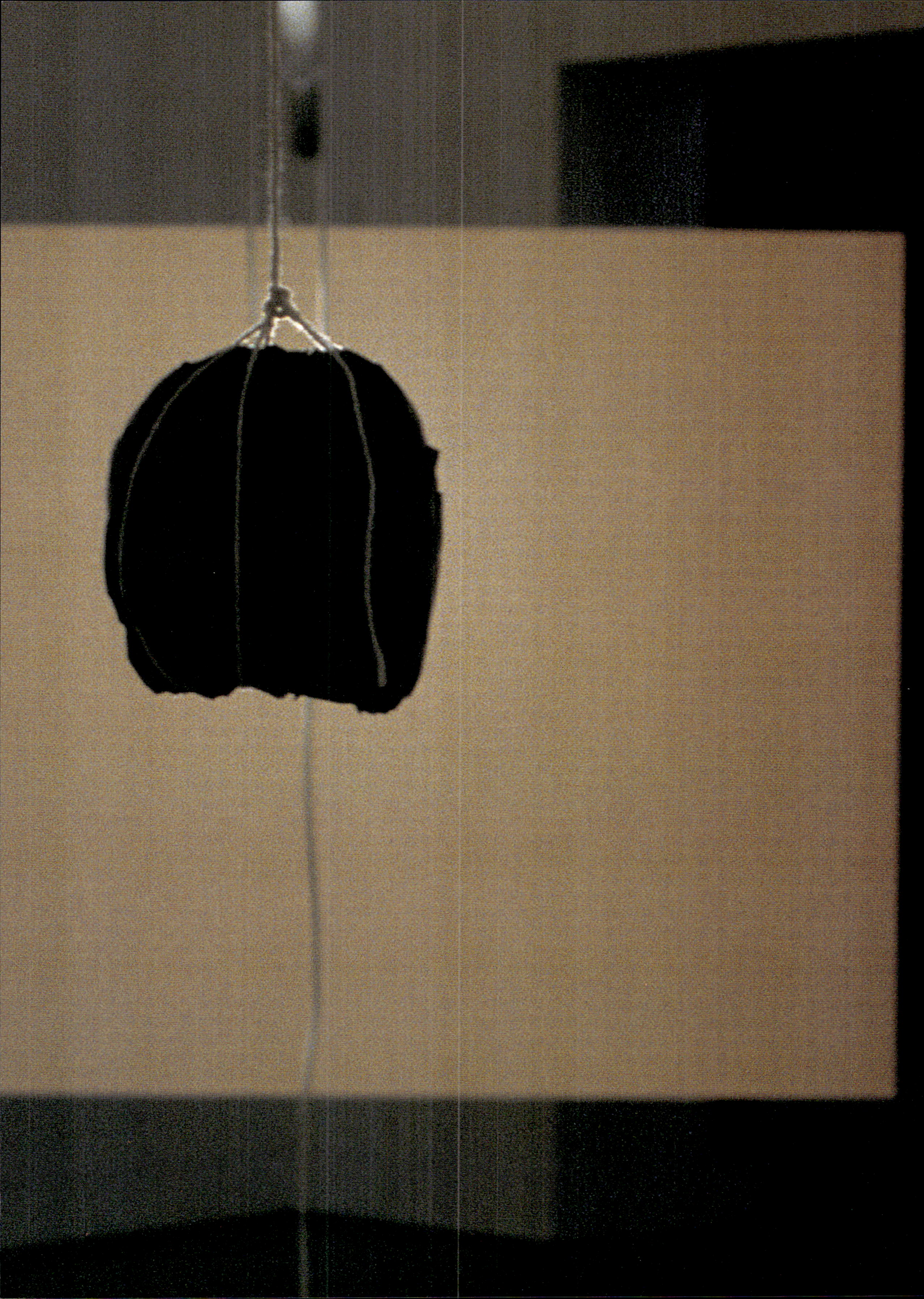

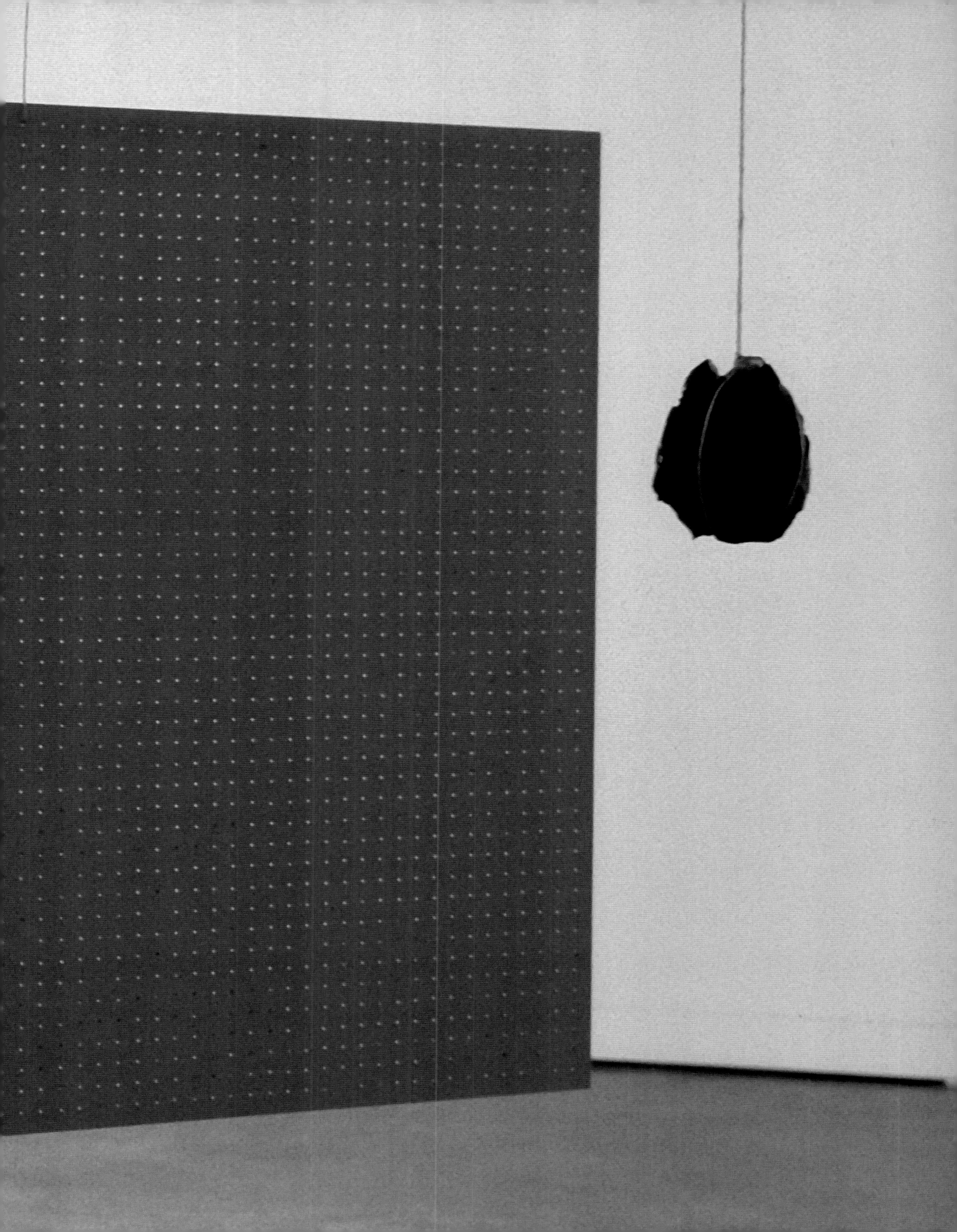

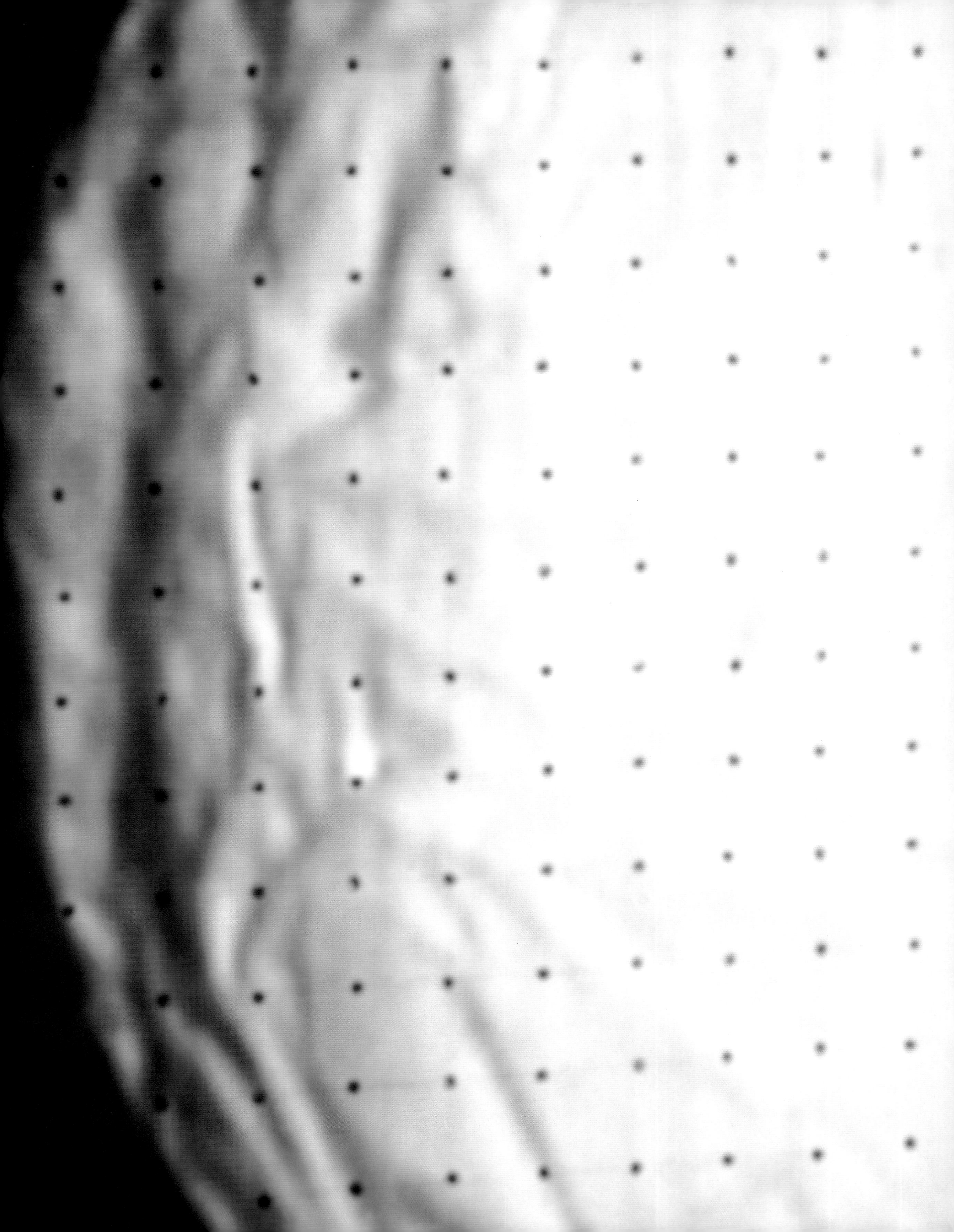

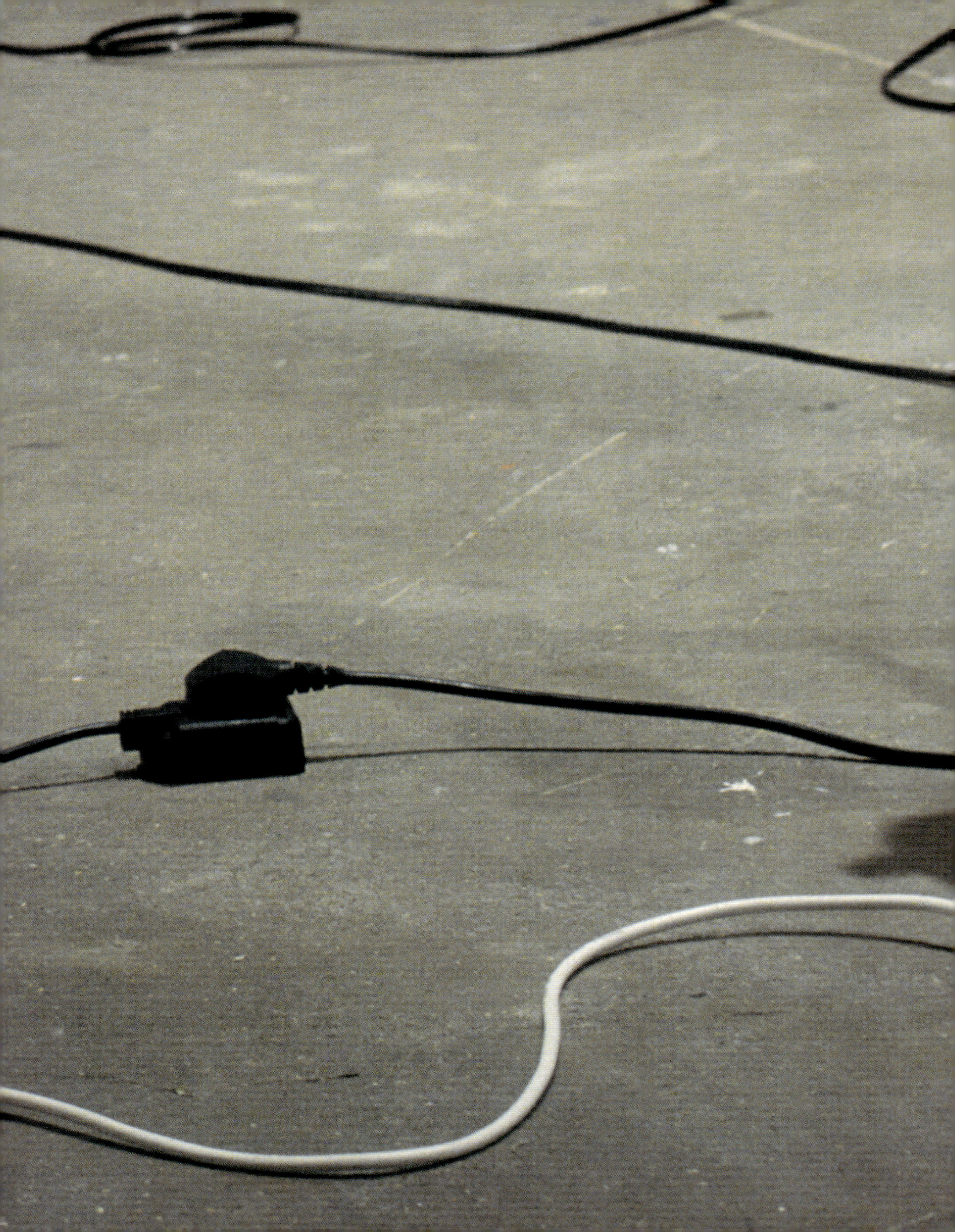

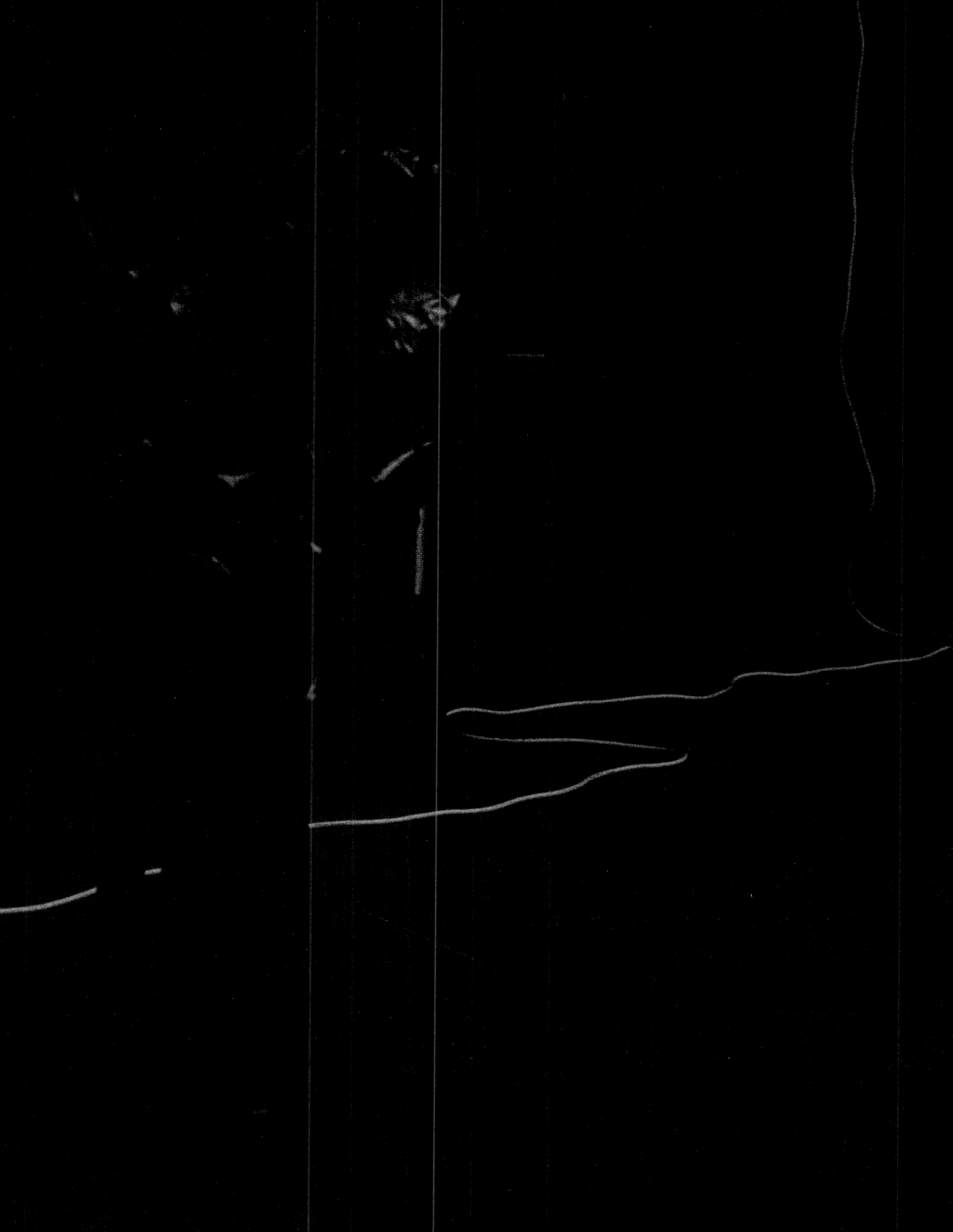

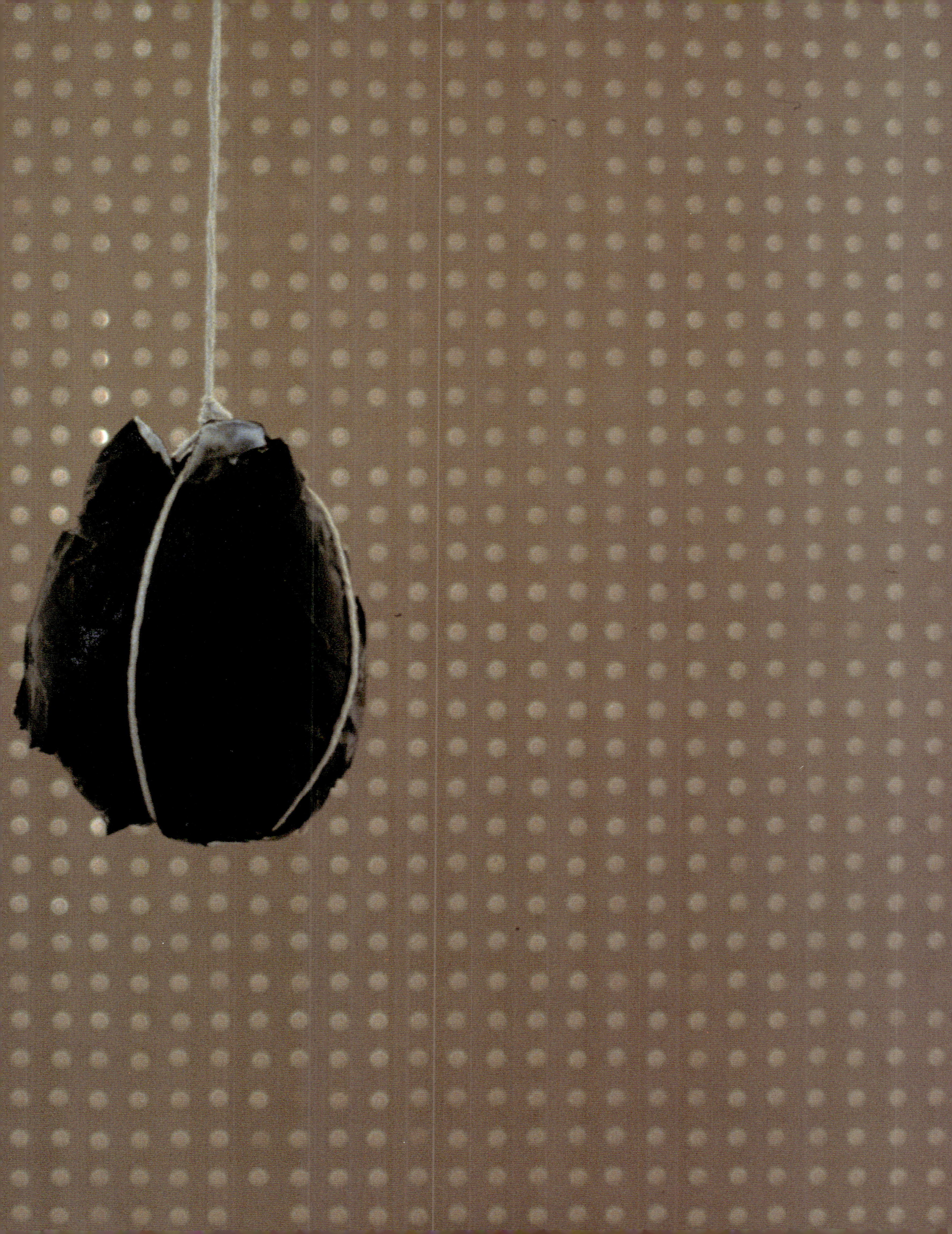

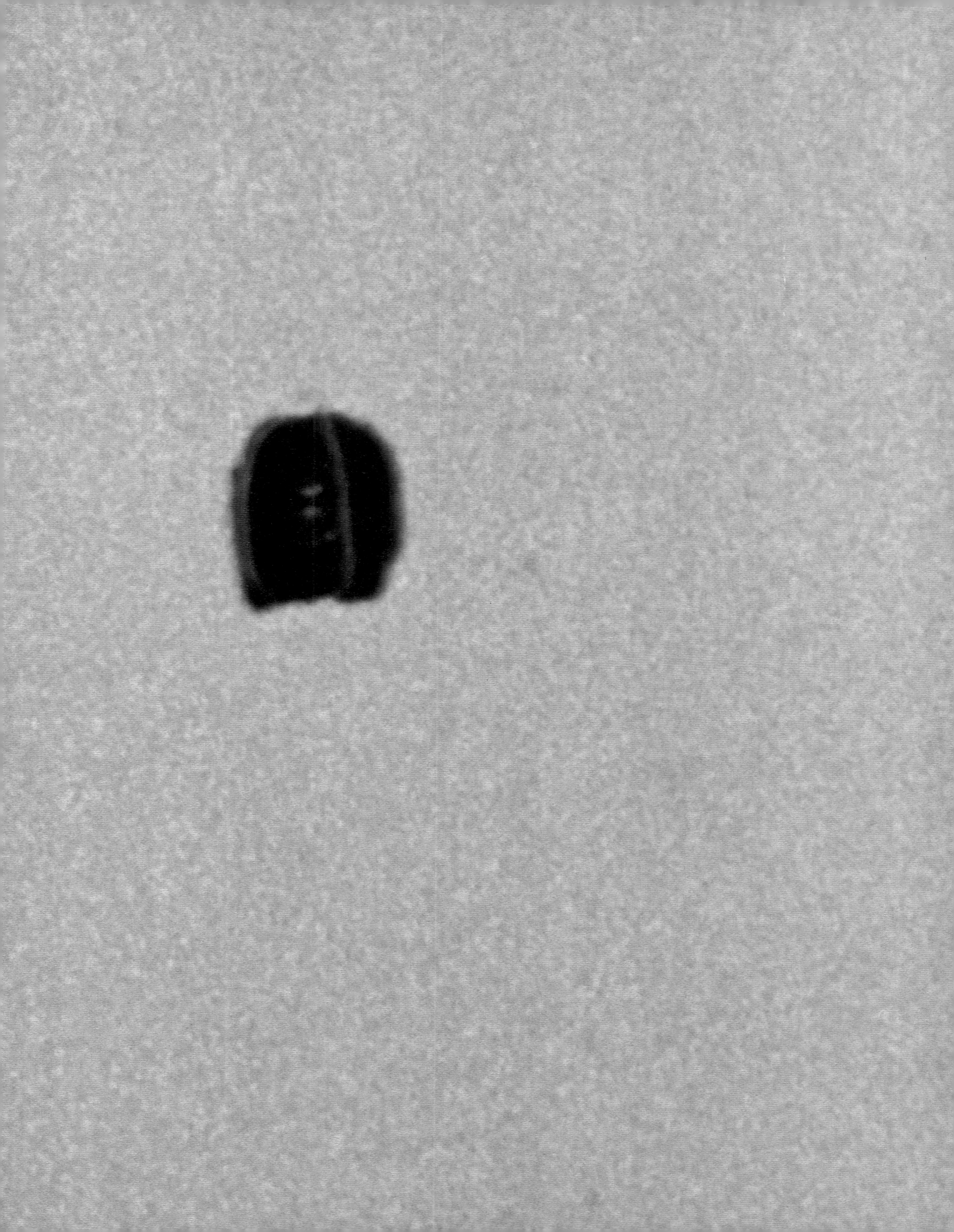

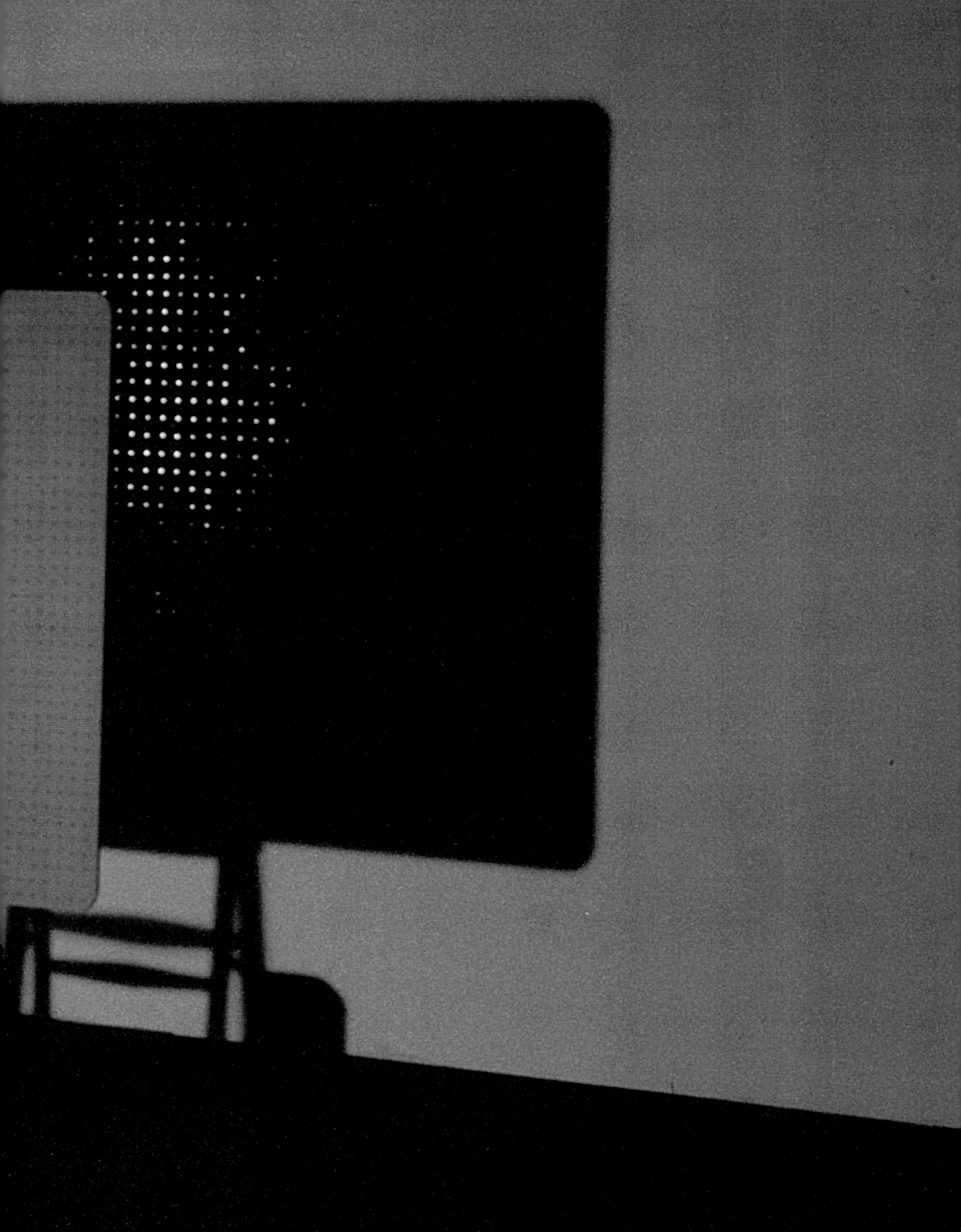

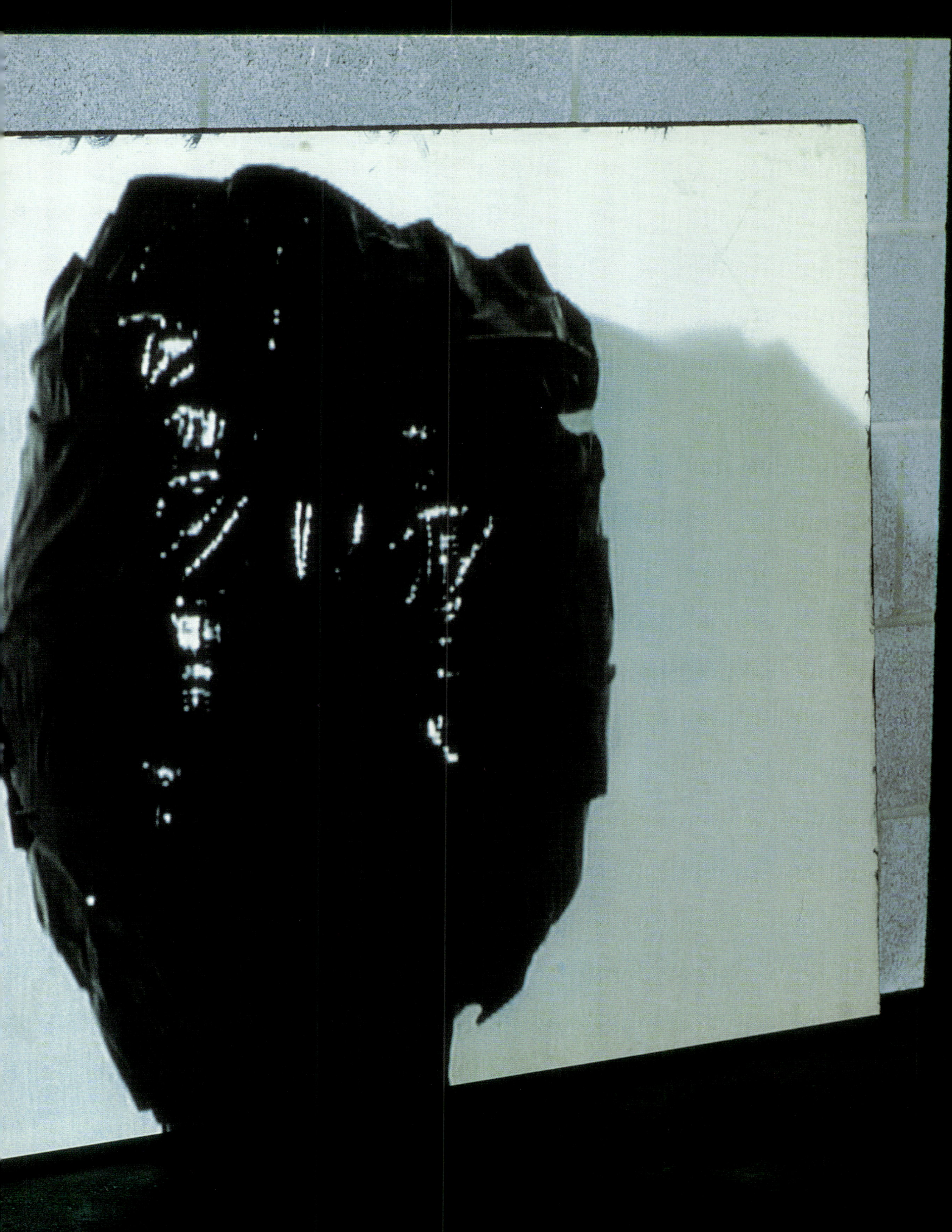

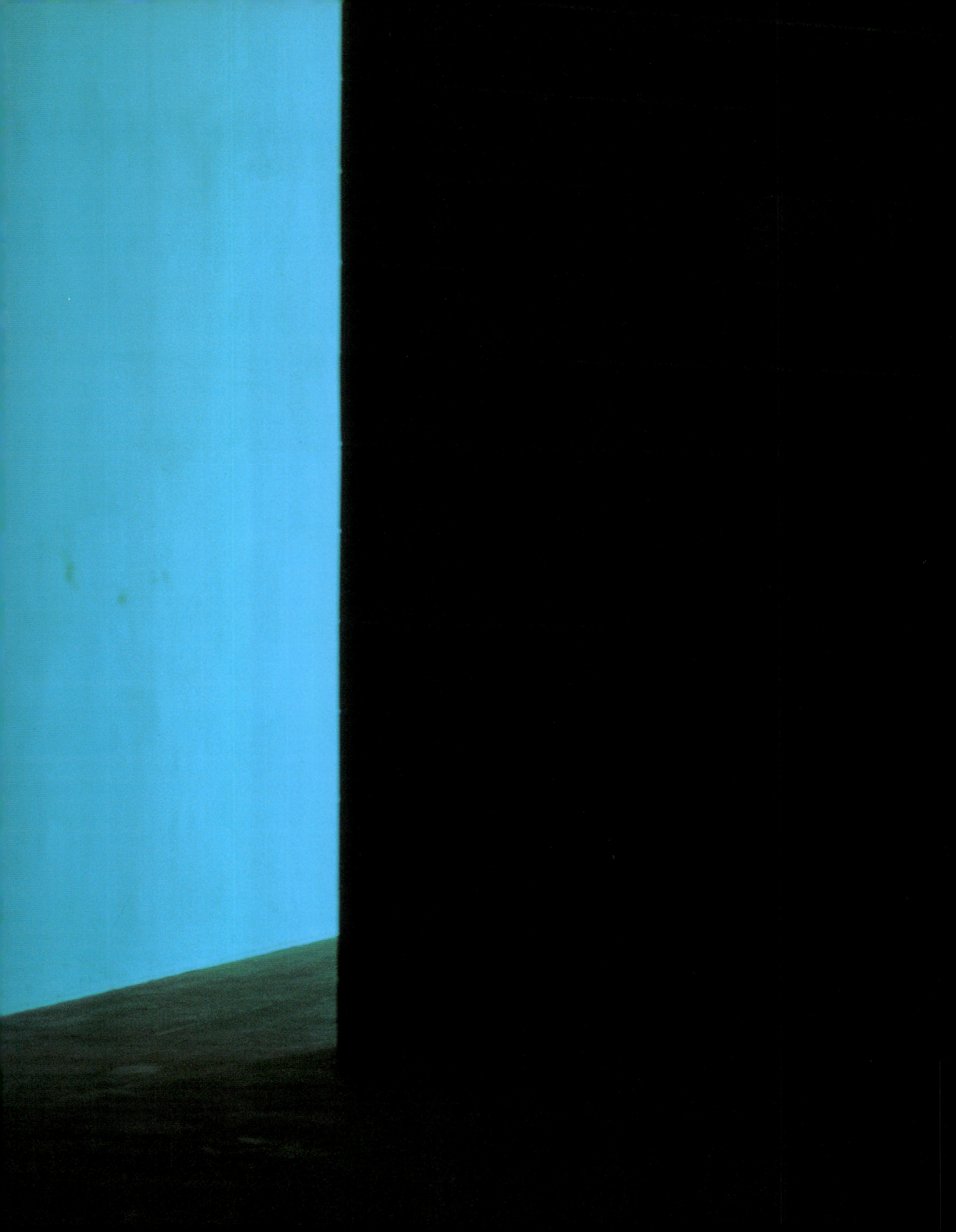

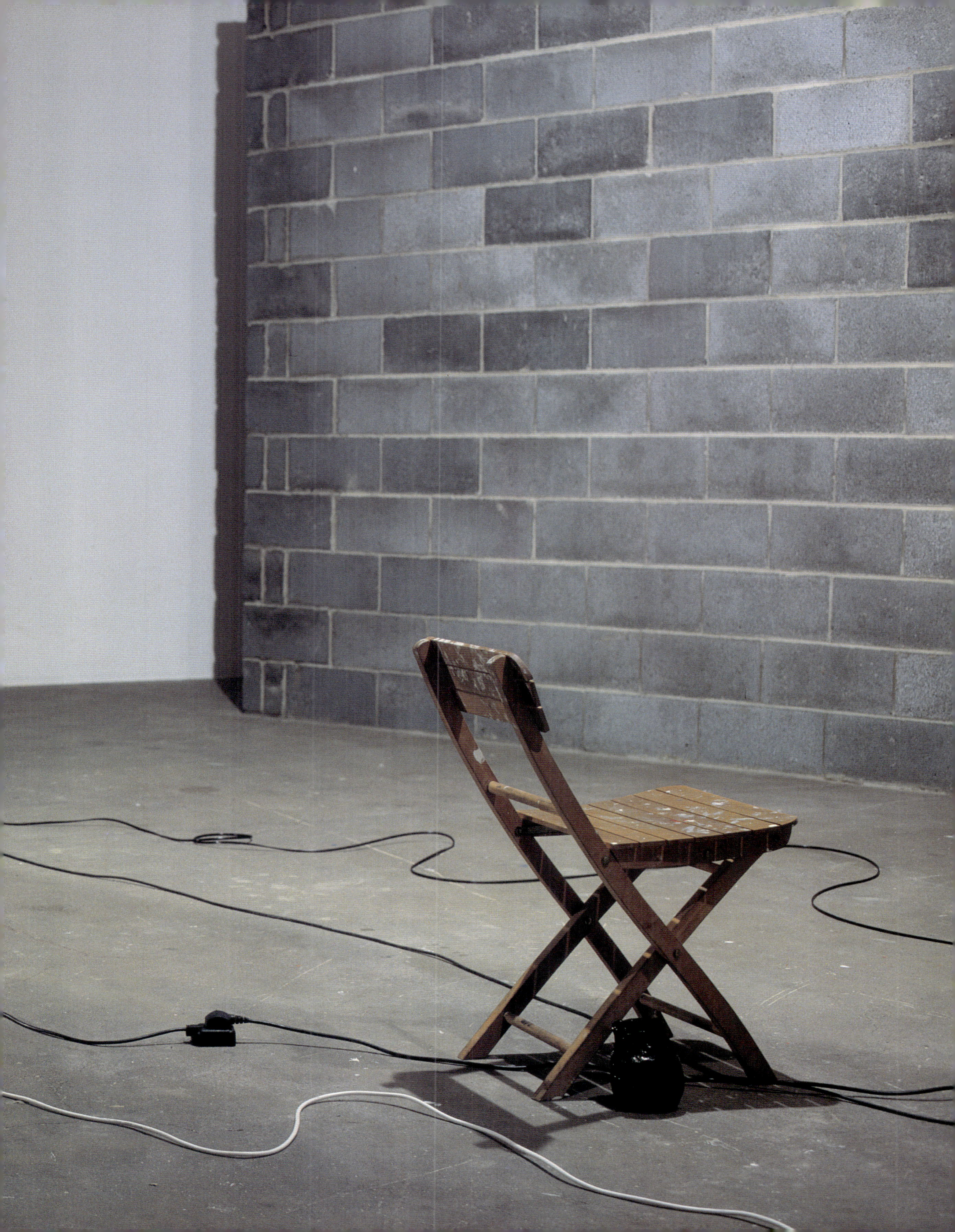

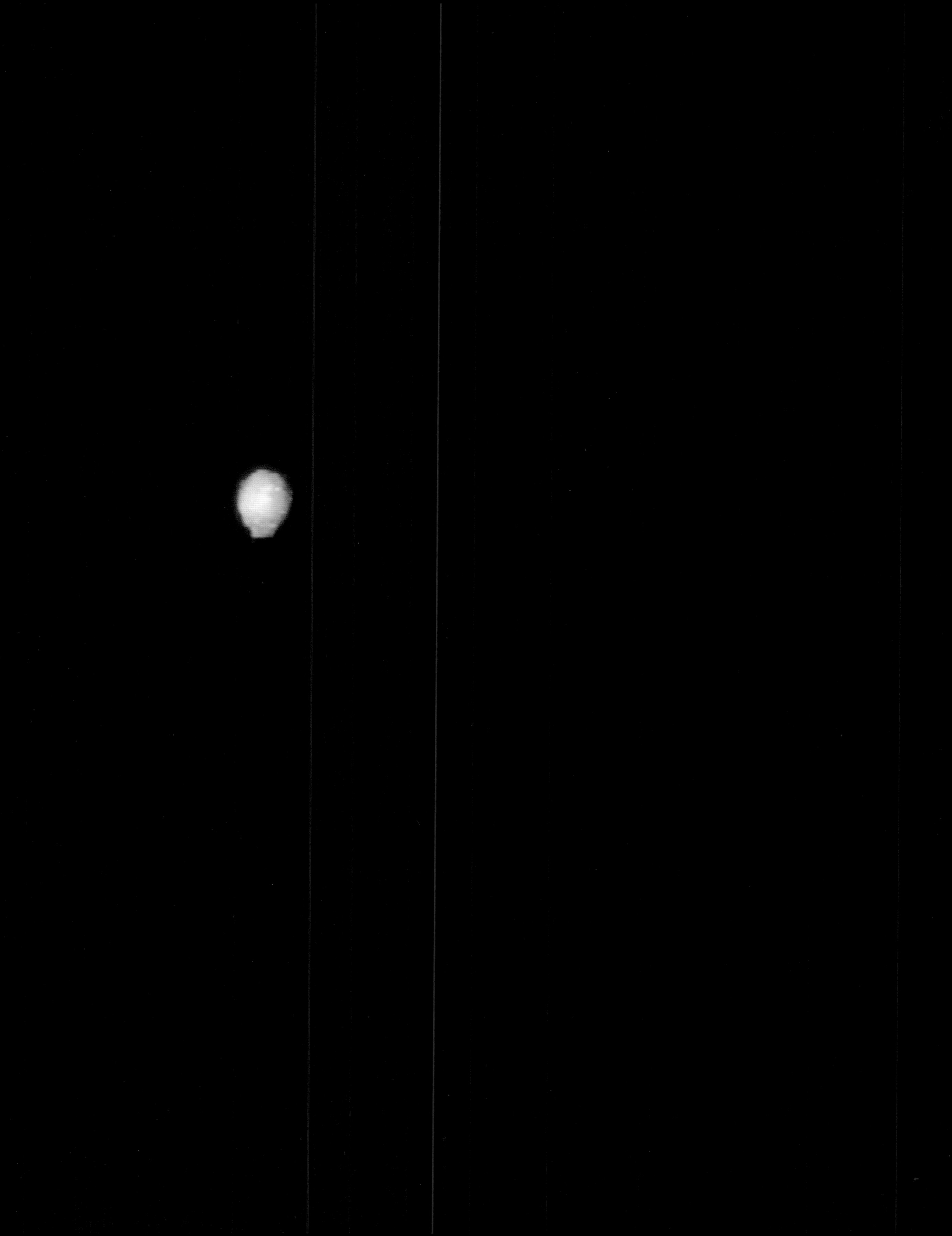

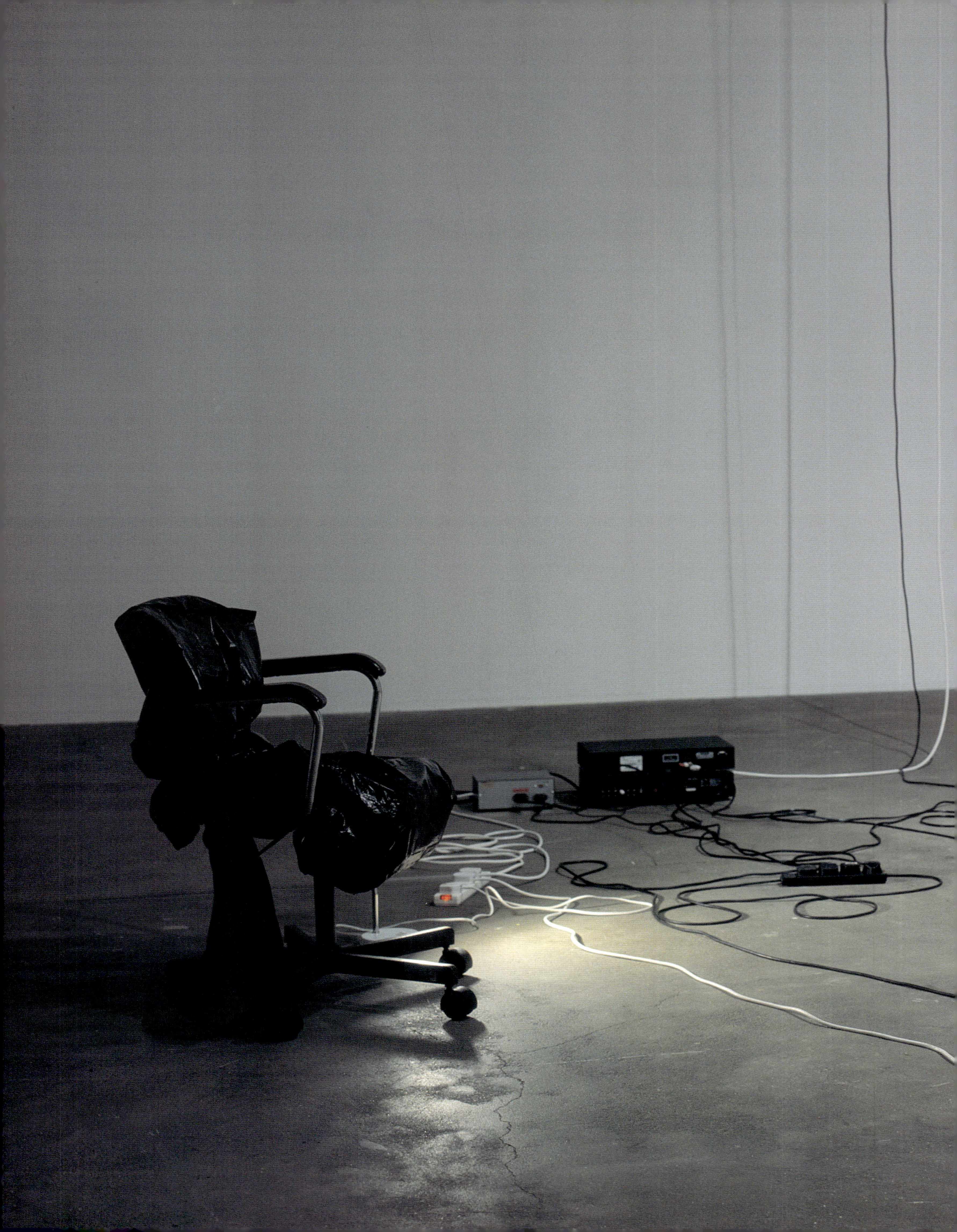

Cloth, Lack and Atrophy

Your kidnappers came for you on a Monday evening. They found you in a bathrobe and alpaca slippers. Your hair was still wet from the shower, your fingers sticky from the home-made pastry you'd been rolling on your kitchen counter. Their faces, distended by the front door's frosted glass, had the viscous look of faces in dreams. You asked your boyfriend to slip the security chain on, but the request was lost among the first words of a woman's frantic account of a car crash outside the flat, then the thumps, your boyfriend's screams, the white girl pointing the pistol at you shouting *Bitch shut up you fucking bitch*, the rifle-butt swinging from the black man's hands towards your face. And when they'd tied you, gagged you, thrown you in the Chevy's boot and pulled out spraying the building and the street with submachine gun fire, it seemed to you that your life, *that* life (the uncooked pie, the essay on Rubens which you'd handed your professor two hours earlier, the unsmoked reefer sitting in the ashtray on the TV, the wedding preparations) had already ended, that *that* you had died outside this car boot door whose inner surface glowed with crimson from the tail lights. Later, though, when you saw your mother wearing black surrounded by reporters on TV, it seemed that she, not you, was dead, that your father standing beside her was dead too, that everything that wasn't where you were was unreal, illusive, dead.

They locked you in a closet for nine weeks: a five-by-five-foot box sound-proofed with pads that smelt of old sweat. On the floor, an untacked, musty carpet and a rubberfoam mattress cancer-eaten by the cigarette-ends and piss of (how many? ten? twenty? a hundred?) people crashed out on floors they never owned in dingy tenements and flophouses. The battered radio they'd placed there with you, which you weren't allowed to turn off or retune, blared out rock and soul all day (and all night too, although you couldn't tell the difference). Occasionally, between the songs, you heard your name being spoken on news bulletins, and heard re-played the taped communiqués you'd been made to record in this very closet, the padded walls now swallowing and muffling their own past. When your captors led you blindfolded to and from the toilet, their voices – men's voices, women's voices, solemn or giggling, colliding and separating around you as you moved unsteadily across the room (rooms?) – were as faceless as the voices on the radio. After a few days the two groups merged: the disc-jockeys and lonely night-time callers became your guards, their voices burrowing beneath the surface of your sleep, hollowing it out until you'd wake up with a start and, peeping through the crack of the closet door, watch the dark shapes of their owners smoking silently beside the windows.

Sometimes they came in and read to you from Engels, Mao and Marx. They told you that your father was a corporate enemy of *the people* and was going to pay *the people* back. Mostly they left you alone for hours and hours on end. On the night of your abduction, when your legs had fought against their arms and dragged across the tarmac, clinging to it as though it could have clamped you, held you back, you'd grazed your knee. Your kidnappers had dressed the wound for you. Now, partly out of boredom and partly because pain was your own, the one thing they couldn't deprive you of unless they killed you, you'd peel back the Band-Aids holding the gauze dressing in place, break the scab and daub the fresh blood into patterns, watching it dry, crack and flow again, scouring its formations for the shapes of animals or continents or figures from paintings you'd studied. You remembered lying on your back looking at clouds. You imagined your knee was the sky and you were God, gazing at the

Let us consider if
we may, gentlemen,
the membrane. Less
an object than an
interval, a buffer,
a relation, the
membrane is no
less palpable for that.
Unguent, mucous and
gelatinous, sheet-like
and pliable, fibrous or
vitreous, translucent or
opaque, the membrane,
when interrogated,
speaks of protozoic
origins. *Involucrum,
glandulae squamosae*
and the folds and striae
of pigment that compose
the *corona ciliaris* of
mosses and ferns; the
pill and piling between
bark and tree; the
dermal expanse of
the sponge; the thin
and soft *conjunctiva
bulbi* spread across
the inside of the eyeball
like a coat of grease
on a ballbearing: all
these proclaim the
membrane.

The membrane
envelops parts, yet
is not one itself. It
packages, gathers
and unifies. Yet at the
same time it divides,
drawing a line between
inside and outside,
the civilised corporeal
polis and the barbarian
ground that lies beyond
its jurisdiction. It is
not the membrane's
lot to merely occupy
this threshold: rather,
it defines the zones on
either side by its own
twists and contortions.
Reflect if you will
upon the jellyfish,
the acalephic zoöid of
the chrysaora family.
Constitutionally
distinguished from

very, very dreadfully nervous I had been and am, but why *will* you say that I am mad? The disease had sharpened my senses – not destroyed – not dulled them. Above all was my sense of hearing acute. I heard all things in the heaven and in the earth. I heard many things in hell. How, then

think it was his eye! yes, it was this! He had the eye of a vulture – a pale blue eye, with a film over it. Whenever it fell upon me, my blood ran cold; and so by degrees – very gradually – I made up my

when I had made an opening sufficient for my head, I put in a dark lantern, all closed, closed, so that no light shone out, and then I thrust in my head. Oh, you would have

undid it just so much that a single thin ray fell upon the vulture eye. And this I did for

moved on the bed suddenly, as if startled. Now you may think that I drew back – but no. His room was as black as pitch with the thick darkness (for the shutters were close fastened, through fear of robbers), and so I knew that he could not see the opening

up in the bed listening;– just as I have done, night after night, hearkening to the death watches

patterns from above, the sky's other side. You imagined you were a photographer and the closet a dark room trickling with warm red light. Negative, positive. At other times you'd slip your fingers through your shirt and feel your heart. You'd hold your breath then hyperventilate to make your heart speed up, so that by lifting your fingers from your chest then lowering them again, breaking and restoring contact, you could play it like a Morse Code tapper, rhythms of beat and silence. Maybe, you thought, the police had sensors that could pick these rhythms up. Maybe they'd seep back into the radio and ride along the air-waves, re-emerging as an interference pattern on some programme. Everything gets picked up and absorbed by something; everything must make some kind of mark.

They demanded, as the terms of your release, that your father's corporation fund a programme for the distribution (*redistribution*) of food to the state's poor (*the people*). Your father replied that to provide every welfare recipient and public housing tenant, not to mention every vagrant, wetback, wino, junky and beggar with a bag of fresh meat, vegetables and tinned food equivalent in value to the sum of seventy dollars as required would cost four hundred million dollars. He offered four. They told him forty. They made you read the previous day's sports results onto another tape to prove that you were still alive, told you they were transferring you to another safehouse, then made you climb into a dustbin which they carried downstairs to a car and placed inside the boot.

Then came the drive: up hills, down hills, along the flat, through traffic and on clear, fast-flowing roads, over tarmac and gravel. In the darkness, rolling and bumping against the dustbin's corrugated sides, you interpreted the journey's texture. You rehearsed in your mind the sequence of jolts, the irregular grinding of the engine and the softness of the ground, the quietness of the air that would signal the car's drawing up in woods. If that happened, it would mean you were being executed: the dustbin would be placed against a tree and peppered with gunfire. You practised contracting your limbs and torso, scrumpling them up into a ball that maybe, just maybe – if they hit the surface of the dustbin not at regularly spaced intervals but following instead some freakish quirk of random distribution coinciding perfectly with your position – would be small enough to fall among the spaces not traversed by bullets. You tried to second-guess the vectors death would take. You imagined the moment when your body would be found by kids on racers or a family on a picnic or a pair of lovers looking for a spot to lie down and disrobe in. You imagined the scene an hour from then: the woods cordoned off and squad cars, ambulances and pathology labs sprawled out untidily beneath the trees, the air whirring and clicking with cameras as investigators marked out and transcribed the elaborate geometry of your limbs' relative positions, the angles of your feet and hands.

In the darkness, rolling and bumping against the dustbin's corrugated sides, you tried to counterbalance the death-scene you'd built up for yourself by picturing the new safehouse you were supposedly being conveyed to: the texture of its closet's carpet and mattress, the smell of its padding. You plotted the path you would follow to the toilet, tried to hear the voices billowing around you. You willed this new place into being and willed the car towards it, relocating it each time you changed direction. You planted rows of shops, restaurants and apartment buildings along the car's route, edging out the vacant lots and scrapyards – proxy woods – that sprung up in your mind from time to time. Parades, gas-stations, woods and lots, parades: as you rolled and bumped inside the dustbin,

the mass through which its sinuous spasms propel it by a factor of less than one percent, this transparent creature feeds by turning itself inside out. Like a rubber glove or ruptured tennis ball it peels back its own exterior and emerges raw and unprotected from its proper domain, evacuates its compound. The sally is as short as it is fruitful: enfolding its food, it involutes once more. In this way, the jellyfish processes space. We could go as far as to say that in breaching and re-establishing its limits, it renders the sea meaningful, allotting status to itself, ocean and void through an act of consumption that always demands a victim.

The membrane locates us, places us in space. It wraps space around us and, in wrapping us, delivers us. Consider the thin and fragile carapace of the automobile hurtling across a landscape. Consider in particular its windscreen. Objects and distances are swallowed and digested by it, distending and disintegrating as its clear, sharp juices break them down. Prisoners in two dimensions, they slide not towards us who sit behind the windscreen but rather across us, simultaneously thrown into motion and arrested by the

in the wall.

Presently I heard a slight groan, and I knew it was the groan of mortal terror. It was not a groan of pain or of grief – oh, no! – it was the low stifled sound that arises from the bottom of the soul when overcharged with awe. I knew the sound well. Many a night, just at midnight, when all the world slept, it has welled up from my own bosom, deepening, with its dreadful echo, the terrors that distracted me. I say I ▮▮▮▮▮▮▮▮▮▮▮▮▮▮▮▮▮▮▮▮▮▮▮▮▮▮▮▮▮▮▮▮▮▮▮▮▮▮▮ *in vain*; because Death, in approaching him had stalked with his black shadow before him, and enveloped the victim. And it was the mournful influence of the unperceived shadow that caused him to feel – although he neither saw nor heard – to *feel* the presence of my head within the room.

▮▮▮▮▮▮▮▮▮▮▮▮▮▮▮▮▮▮▮▮▮▮▮▮▮▮▮▮▮▮▮▮▮▮▮▮▮▮▮ a low, dull, quick sound, such as a watch makes when enveloped in cotton. I knew *that* sound well, too. It was the beating of the old man's heart. It increased my fury, as the beating of a drum stimulates the soldier into ▮▮▮▮▮▮▮▮▮▮▮▮▮▮▮▮▮▮▮▮▮▮▮▮▮▮▮▮▮▮▮▮▮▮▮ anxiety seized me – the sound would be heard by a neighbour! The old man's hour had come! With a loud yell, I threw open the lantern and leaped into ▮▮▮▮▮▮ dragged him to the floor, and pulled the heavy ▮▮▮▮▮▮ with a muffled sound. ▮▮▮▮▮▮▮▮▮▮▮▮▮▮▮▮▮▮▮▮▮▮▮▮▮▮▮▮▮

possible worlds jostled for position on the outside, each preparing itself for inhabitation. When, finally, your captors hauled you out and led you up a staircase to a room in which music was playing, liver sizzling in a pan, a TV cackling, people talking, you threw back your head and laughed, then stepped across the threshold of your new closet like a bride returning from her honeymoon to take charge of a newly-purchased dream home. You placed your shoes on first one shelf and then another, chose the best position for the radio, fluffed up the pillow, felt the familiar pockmarked rhythms of the mattress, gasped in the old smell of the blanket – laughing all the time not from relief but from a growing sense of power: immense, primordial power stemming from the knowledge that it wasn't you that fitted into the universe but universes that took shape around you like filings around a magnet, footballers around a ball or ripples around a stone dropped into water.

After a few days your kidnappers came for you again. Finding you too weak to walk, they locked their arms beneath your legs and carried you like a king out of the closet to the living room where, slipping off your blindfold from behind, they showed you scenes of chaos being enacted in your name. On the TV, food distributions were turning into riots as a hail of eggs and frozen turkey giblets rained down on three separate cities. Windows were smashing, car hulks burning, sky and pavement tumbling round and jumping up towards the camera as the newsmen ran for cover from the watercannons' jets. And *thirty thousand people! thirty thousand people* had been fed, they kept announcing – your kidnappers, the various channels' anchormen and commentators, spokesmen from your father's corporation. *Six times more than Jesus!* Is it here that your conversion has its roots? Did the old you die and get reborn? Was it ideology that converted you? Or was it love that brought you over to their side? And then, for whom? For them? *The people?* In your next taped communiqué you described how your love had *grown now to embrace everyone: my comrades here, in prison, on the streets.* You denounced your father as *a pig*, and outlined a dystopia of automated industry lurking five years into the future, the state a giant machine reducing citizens to button-pushing servants. You called upon *the people* to express their words of freedom with their guns. Perhaps it was this vision that seduced you: life as violence, life as struggle, armoured carriers criss-crossing city streets, the smell of cordite, black smoke billowing against the daylight sky, the sound of Tommy-guns and snipers' rifles, house-searches confounded by false walls and hidden basements, barbed wire closing off whole sections of the city, the commonness of death.

You robbed a bank: heiress, debutante, art A-student, urban guerilla. The closed-circuit television camera caught it: how you vaulted the partition, planted your legs firmly on the floor and raised your gun up to your waist. *I'll blow your motherfucking heads away!* you said. Your own head was light, drunk on clear blue daylight and real, untinned air. As you were driven to the heist, the streets that slid by kinked and wrinkled in window of your car. Traffic lights and stop signs were outlandish, shopfronts an unreal sea of colours and reflections. As you left the bank, one of your comrades opened fire and glass cascaded down across the bodies quivering on the floor. Dazed, you lowered your gun and glided to the car. You fixed your gaze onto the rear view mirror as you sped away, to stop yourself from throwing up. In it you saw what every other surface – mirror, television, window, dream – would show you from now on: a world retreating from you, at high speed, into a screen.

aggressive film poured and hardened in our furnaces and assembly lines. Insects come to grief across this gauze more messily: the best that they can hope for is to leave a smear, a stain, a patch – a record of their own untimely and untidy end.

Receiving, storing and relaying, the membrane is the very stuff of history. It is the pulp and the papyrus, census-taker and town crier, the still-wet, submissive vinyl waiting to be scored and the hard disc through whose unyielding, obstacle-filled groove the needle drags and catches, making loud-speakers vibrate. It is the hide or parchment stretched across the tom-tom; hit the membrane and it will declaim you.

Should we describe as active or passive this paradox which, inviting violence, responds with a *j'accuse!*? The eyes of dead men have been known to photo-graph their murderers. This, though, is rare: eyelids, in general, prefer to act as shutters, or shells if you like, imposing separation and affording solace, like a safety curtain in a theatre, ready to be drawn in case the drama grows too visceral.

But gentlemen, these lights are bright and I sense your attention wandering. Let us repair, if we may, to continue these deliberations elsewhere.

precautions I took for the concealment of the body. The

knocking at the street door. I went down to open it with a light heart, – for what had I *now* to fear? There entered three men, who introduced themselves, with perfect suavity, as officers of the police. A shriek had been heard by a

for *what* had I to fear? I bade the gentlemen welcome. The shriek, I said, was my own in a dream. The old man, I mentioned, was absent in the country. I took my visitors

were satisfied. My *manner* had convinced them. I was singularly at ease. They sat, and while I answered cheerily, they chatted of familiar
myself getting pale and wished them gone. My head ached, and I fancied a ringing in my ears: but still they sat and still chatted.

not within my ears.

low, dull, quick sound – much such a sound as a watch makes when enveloped in cotton.

paced the floor to and fro with heavy strides, as if

swung the chair upon which I had been sitting, and grated it upon the boards, but the noise arose over all and continually increased. It grew louder – louder – *louder!* And still the men

derision! I could bear those hypocritical smiles no longer! I felt that I must scream or die! and now – again! – hark!

shrieked, 'dissemble no more! I admit the deed! – tear up the planks! here, here! – it is the beating of his

Smith/Stewart
A Black Thread
A Film and Video Umbrella touring exhibition,
supported by the National Touring Programme of Arts Council England
and The Henry Moore Foundation

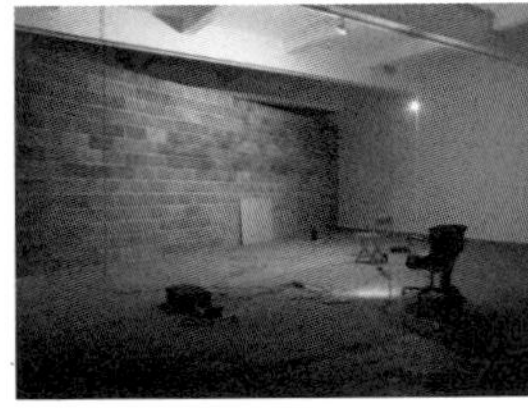

A Black Thread
Chisenhale Gallery, London
6 November – 15 December 2002
Commissioned in collaboration with Chisenhale Gallery

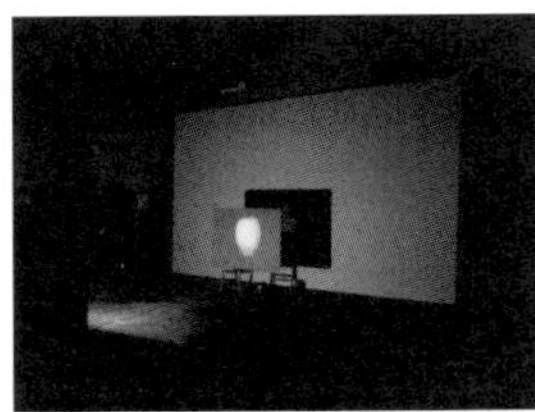

A Black Thread 2
Fletcher Works, Sheffield
29 March – 19 April 2003
Commissioned in collaboration with Site Gallery, Sheffield as part of Art Sheffield 03

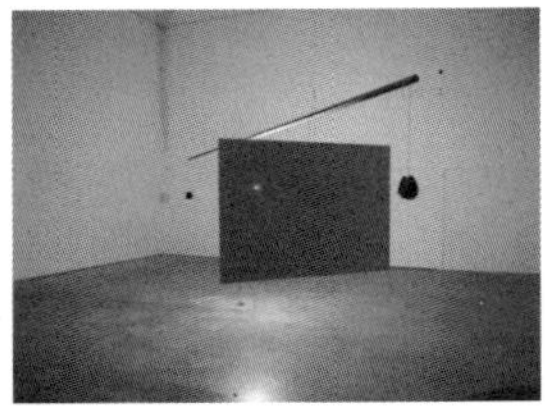

A Black Thread (part three)
Together yet apart
Mirrored but not
Milton Keynes Gallery
31 January – 21 March 2004
Commissioned in collaboration with Milton Keynes Gallery

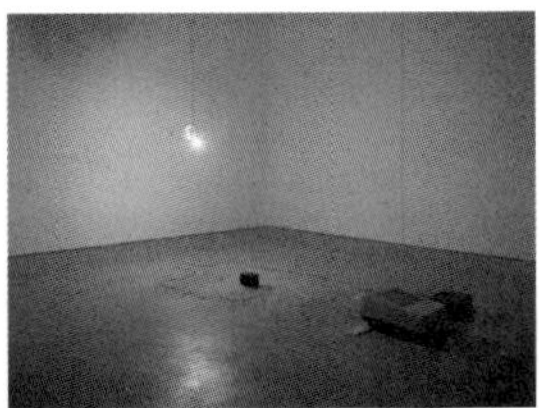

A Black Thread
Published by Film and Video Umbrella, in association with Milton Keynes Gallery,
with thanks to the School of Fine Art, Glasgow School of Art

Edited by Steven Bode
Designed by Richard Bonner-Morgan
Printed by Trichrom Limited
Texts by Tom McCarthy, including extracts from 'The Tell-Tale Heart' by Edgar Allan Poe
Installation photographs by Smith/Stewart

Smith/Stewart would like to thank:
The Smiths and the Stewarts; Steven Bode, Mike Jones, Caroline Smith, Nina Ernst, Bevis Bowden and
Keith Whittle at Film and Video Umbrella; John Gill, Hannah Kruse, Stuart Croft and all staff at Chisenhale Gallery;
Jeanine Griffin, Carol Maund and the installation team at Site Gallery; Stephen Snoddy, Emma Dean,
Emma Gregory and all staff at Milton Keynes Gallery; Tom McCarthy; Richard Bonner-Morgan;
Adrian Fogarty; Charlotte Nourse; Malcolm Bailey and the A10 team, UMIST, Manchester

Printed in an edition of 1,000
ISBN 1-90427-008-5
©2004, Film and Video Umbrella, the artists and the authors

Film and Video Umbrella 52 Bermondsey Street London SE1 3UD
Tel 020 7407 7755 Fax 020 7407 7766 Email info@fvu.co.uk

Milton Keynes Gallery 900 Midsummer Boulevard Central Milton Keynes MK9 3QA
Tel 01908 676 900 Fax 01908 558 308 Email info@mk-g.org

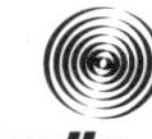
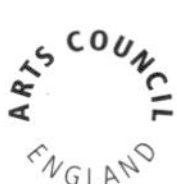

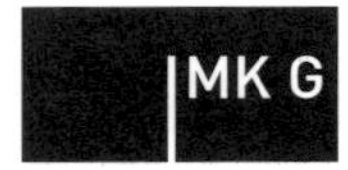

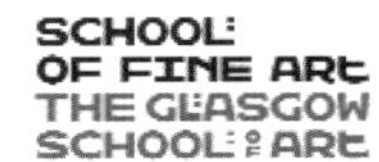

film and video umbrella